Teaching is a zero-sum game. If it's not adding to the learning, it's subtracting from it.

Peps Mccrea

Brilliant Behaviour in 60 Seconds or Less

Teaching becomes much harder when students misbehave. This book provides over 100 evidence-based strategies to help teachers effectively manage student behaviour and improve the quality of teaching and learning.

Written by leading expert Robin Launder (the Behaviour Buddy), it outlines the routines that underpin effective behaviour management, the expectations that need to be set and how to achieve student buy-in through little nuggets of tried-and-tested teacher wisdom that you can use in your classroom straightaway. Each tip takes about a minute to read, and collectively they will set up the conditions for brilliant behaviour for the entire academic year. The chapters cover:

- The teacher–student relationship
- Improving your presence and clarity
- Embedding routines
- Attention grabbers
- Strategic corrections
- Successful sanctions
- Follow-up conversations

Breaking behaviour management down into a series of practical steps, this is essential reading for every teacher. It doesn't matter if you're new to the profession or experienced, primary or secondary, state or independent, UK or non-UK; if you're a teacher, then this book is for you.

Robin Launder is a consultant and trainer specialising in behaviour management. He has taught in primary, secondary and special schools, and in the state and private sectors. He also has a background in psychiatry, therapeutic communities and prisons. Robin has written for several education publications and has developed online behaviour management courses for teachers and teaching assistants. For more information, go to www.behaviourbuddy.co.uk.

Brilliant Behaviour in 60 Seconds or Less

Tried and Tested Strategies for Teachers

Robin Launder

LONDON AND NEW YORK

Designed cover image: © Getty Images

First published 2026
by Routledge
4 Park Square, Milton Park, Abingdon, Oxon OX14 4RN

and by Routledge
605 Third Avenue, New York, NY 10158

Routledge is an imprint of the Taylor & Francis Group, an informa business

© 2026 Robin Launder

The right of Robin Launder to be identified as author of this work has been asserted in accordance with sections 77 and 78 of the Copyright, Designs and Patents Act 1988.

All rights reserved. No part of this book may be reprinted or reproduced or utilised in any form or by any electronic, mechanical, or other means, now known or hereafter invented, including photocopying and recording, or in any information storage or retrieval system, without permission in writing from the publishers.

Trademark notice: Product or corporate names may be trademarks or registered trademarks, and are used only for identification and explanation without intent to infringe.

British Library Cataloguing-in-Publication Data
A catalogue record for this book is available from the British Library

ISBN: 978-1-041-00054-9 (hbk)
ISBN: 978-1-041-00050-1 (pbk)
ISBN: 978-1-003-60799-1 (ebk)

DOI: 10.4324/9781003607991

Typeset in Optima
by codeMantra

Contents

	About the Author	ix
	Preface	x
	Introduction: Conformity	1
1	Super Tips	5
2	Relationship Rules	10
3	Presence and Clarity	16
4	The Fundamentals	23
5	Embed Routines	34
6	Key Routines	39
7	Attention Grabbers	51
8	Strategic Corrections	55
9	Successful Sanctions	65

Contents

10	Follow-Up Conversation	68
11	Managing the Challenging	74
12	Never-Evers	80
13	Unconscious Processes	88
14	Turn the Class Around	97
	Further Support	*101*

About the Author

Did poorly at school. Nearly expelled. Didn't get any O Levels. Did nothing for a couple of years. Joined the Prison Service. Seconded to train as a psychiatric nurse and psychodynamic counsellor. Delivered serious offender programmes. Left the Prison Service with a long-service medal in hand. Became an English and drama teacher (but had to get maths GCSE first). Worked as a School Improvement Partner. Taught in a Pupil Referral Unit. Set up an own business – Behaviour Buddy. Created online behaviour management programmes. Wrote this book. Phew!

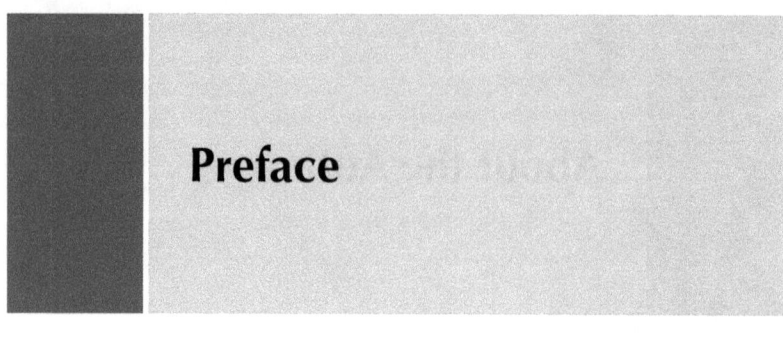

Preface

Every week for approaching a decade now, I've emailed behaviour management tips to any teacher who wants them – that's thousands of emails to colleagues working across all educational settings and phases. Many have told me how helpful they find my tips (thank you!), and a good number have asked whether I'd collate them into a single book for ease of access.

So I have. And you are reading it now.

I've given the tips a light edit and sorted them into chapters, but otherwise they're the same 'nuggets of behaviour wisdom' (to quote one teacher) as before. I've also added a title. The '60 Seconds or Less' bit refers to the average time it will take to read each tip. I'm being a bit tongue-in-cheek of course, but nevertheless I've tried to make my writing as concise and precise as possible. As we know, the easier something is to understand, the easier it is to do.

Two terminology points. First, I've plumped for 'student' over 'pupil' or 'learner'. Nothing wrong with those other terms, but I had to choose one so 'student' it is. Second, this is how I define the concept of 'misbehaviour':

> Any student behaviour that gets in the way of learning.

Preface

It's a useful definition because it's simple and non-judgemental and keeps the focus where it needs to be – namely, on student learning.

You'll find over a hundred tried-and-tested tips in this book. Most tips will work with most students in most contexts most of the time. That said, you should make reasonable adjustments where necessary. This is particularly the case for students with special educational needs. Don't let the tips become an ideology, but instead use them as a tool.

I've also included two additional chapters: one considers the influence of unconscious processes on student behaviour, and the other gives a step-by-step guide for turning a class around should misbehaviour become the norm. There's also a short section on further support that gives information about my online behaviour management courses, Continuing Professional Development provision and conference talks.

I hang on desperately to the shoulders of giants, not least Paul Dix, Tom Bennett and, towering about them all, Bill Rogers. If you want to delve deeper into the world of behaviour management, look in their direction. Two other fabulous educators are Doug Lemov and Peps Mccrea; respectively, they have written the best book and the best series of books I know about teaching.

I hope you find value in my book, too. If you think of improvements or further tips for inclusion, do let me know. You'd be doing me and future readers a favour.

Robin
robin@behaviourbuddy.co.uk

Introduction: Conformity

There is a phenomenon that every teacher needs to know about. It's central to our role as educators, influences most of what happens in our lessons and is the most powerful force we can leverage in the classroom. It also informs every chapter and most of the tips in this book. The phenomenon is conformity.

Conformity is the tendency to align your behaviour so that you fit in with those around you. That alignment can be a conscious choice, but often it's an unconscious process that happens below the level of awareness. Either way, it's driven by a need to belong, an innate setting hardwired over millions of years of evolution. When we belong, we get the support and safety of the group; when we don't belong, we are isolated and vulnerable. In evolutionary terms, being an outsider is risky, and hence, we are driven to conform.

Conformity, of course, is not an intrinsically good thing. It links with passivity and complacency, and acts against curiosity, creativity and independent thought. Yet, in the classroom, it is a prerequisite for brilliant student behaviour. If students are conforming to your appropriate expectations, that is, if they are behaving in pro-social and pro-learning ways, then the classroom can function as it should. Simply put, conformity creates the conditions for students to flourish.

Brilliant Behaviour in 60 Seconds or Less

Conformity consists of three levers:

- Social norms.
- Social proof.
- Leader buy-in.

Let's look at each in turn.

Social Norms

A social norm is the group's accepted standard of behaviour. It's how group members normally behave when they are together, and sometimes even when they're apart. Norms can be codified into formal rules though most exist as informal understandings. Either way, they are a powerful force that tends to shape and maintain human behaviour in predictable ways.

In the classroom setting, an effective norm is a standardised behaviour that the students readily follow. In the main, this equates to classroom routines, that is, those set and sequenced expectations that tell students what to do, how to do it and when to do it. Routines are a core element of effective behaviour management, and for that reason, this book devotes two chapters to the topic: **Embed Routines** (Chapter 5) and **Key Routines** (Chapter 6). Simply put, when you get routines right, you get a great deal of student behaviour right, too.

Social Proof

Social proof means using the behaviour of others as a way of determining how to behave. We conclude that if others are doing it, then it is probably right or expected that we do it, too.

For students, social proof is peer behaviour. It's what they can see or hear other students doing. If that behaviour is appropriate, then

Introduction: Conformity

they'll be more likely to behave well; but if it's inappropriate, then misbehaviour is the more likely outcome. Certainly, there will be students who can resist peer pressure (in either direction), but most will align to what their peers are doing.

Social proof also comes from the teacher. If the teacher repeatedly draws attention to misbehaviour – *Don't do that! Shhh! How many times have you been told!* – then social proof is leveraged in an unhelpful way. But if they repeatedly highlight appropriate behaviour, then it's helpful. We will return to this idea when we look at **Narrate Compliance** (Tip 25).

Leader Buy-In

Classrooms contain multiple groups. Some will be alliances just for the lesson, whereas others will reach across the school and can even last a lifetime. For classroom behaviour to be optimal, however, there must be a single dominant group and you must lead it. If there is a counter group with greater dominance, then your students will feel pressure to align with its expectations, not yours. At best, some of your students will stay quietly on the sidelines; at worst, you'll lose control of the entire class.

Luckily, and overwhelmingly, students want and expect you to be the leader in the classroom. They readily take on the role of follower because that's the role they're used to – it's their normalised social position as a child and a student. But you can also enhance student buy-in by *acting* as a leader, that is, by conveying confidence, projecting presence and taking charge. If you do those three things, and if you add in the qualities of pleasantness and politeness, you'll be a teacher the students will want to follow.

I wish it didn't matter. I wish that buy-in was solely a product of your standing as an adult and an educator. But it's not, at least not entirely and certainly not sufficiently. Leadership is something you have to create and convey. For that reason, the importance of leadership informs much of this book, not least **Relationship Rules** (Chapter 2), **Presence and Clarity** (Chapter 3) and **Strategic Corrections** (Chapter 8).

One Other Thing ...

So that's the three levers of conformity: social norms, social proof and leader buy-in. The teachers who are best at behaviour management pull on all three at the same time, and they do so consistently and unfailingly. All the tips that now follow, from Chapter 1 through to Chapter 12, will show you how to do that effectively. Make sure too that you read Chapter 13. It does not contain any actual behaviour management tips, but it does look at several unconscious processes and how those processes underpin specific tips within this book.

1 Super Tips

The first five tips in this book are the most important of all. They are broad in scope and foundational in nature, underpinning and knitting together all the tips that follow. These tips – let's call them super tips – are what the teachers who are best at behaviour management do. They might not know that they do them, but they do them anyway.

Tip 1. Behaviour Management Practitioner

Geography teachers have two subjects: geography *and* behaviour management. Science teachers have up to four subjects: the three core sciences *and* behaviour management. And primary school teachers have a million and one subjects: the million subjects that is the primary curriculum *and* behaviour management.

In other words, behaviour management is integral to teaching. Consequently, you must view yourself as a behaviour management practitioner. In fact, more than that, you must embrace the role because when you do you put student behaviour at the forefront of your thinking.

Brilliant Behaviour in 60 Seconds or Less

Behaviour management practitioners don't wing it. They don't leave it to chance and simply hope that the students will behave for them. Instead, they plan for, promote and normalise the behaviour they want. They're also quick to correct any behaviour they don't want, and they do so calmly, efficiently and effectively.

It's a skilled role – so skilled, in fact, that hardly anyone (if anyone) comes into teaching an expert from day one. It takes time, effort and practice to get behaviour right. Yet, the teachers who get it right the quickest are those who embrace the role. When you see yourself as a *Behaviour Management Practitioner*, you think and act like one, and that makes all the difference in the classroom.

Tip 2. Consistently High Expectations

You must have consistently high expectations of all your students – that's academic, behavioural and social expectations (social expectations being how the students interact with you and each other).

High expectations tell your students that you fully believe they have what it takes to achieve, behave and interact in the ways they should. Low expectations convey the opposite, that they can't achieve, can't behave and can't get along with each other.

But how can you know if your expectations are genuinely high? After all, every teacher you'll ever meet will tell you they have high expectations, yet expectations between teachers can vary wildly.

Here's what you do. In any given situation, you imagine what the *best* possible student behaviour looks like and you make that your expectation. Whether it's students entering the classroom, following instructions, paying attention, answering questions, working in pairs, working in fours, doing homework and so on, you imagine the best and you aim squarely for that.

Here's the key point: high or low, behaviour moves in the direction of the expectation, so keep your expectations consistently high.

Tip 3. 100% Rule

Make the following your constant aspirational target:

100% of your students working 100% of the time with 100% engagement.

The closer you get to meeting the 100% Rule, the closer you get to achieving brilliant behaviour. First, it's not possible to work hard and misbehave at the same time. Brains can't multitask in that way. Second, the rule reduces the appeal of misbehaviour. If a student wants to misbehave but everyone else is working, then they'll be less likely to bother. And even if they do bother, their peers will be less likely to join in. Third, the 100% Rule prompts compliance through social proof (see **Introduction: Conformity**). In other words, they see their peers working hard and so follow suit.

There's also another benefit. When you add in good teaching and challenging work, your students will (almost certainly) make excellent progress. And when they do, they'll buy into you more as their teacher. They'll know that their success is down to you. Yes, they're the ones working hard and thinking deeply, but that's because you've created the conditions for that to happen. Their progress comes from your push.

Most importantly of all, the 100% Rule becomes a social norm (see **Introduction: Conformity**). It won't happen overnight, but it will happen over time and often more quickly than you think. However, you must be unrelenting in its pursuit. You can't simply wish for it; you have to work for it, lesson in, lesson out. But when it is in place, when the rule is a fixed feature of your classroom culture, appropriate behaviour becomes self-reinforcing: the students work hard in your lessons because in your lessons they work hard.

Tip 4. Withitness

The term 'withitness' was coined by Jacob Kounin in the late 1960s.[1] It refers to teacher awareness, specifically these three elements. The withit teacher:

- Knows (or has a good idea) what their students are doing at any given time.
- Knows (or has a good idea) what their students will do in any given situation.
- Conveys their awareness of the above to their students.

Withitness comes from closely observing the students, thinking about what you see and registering patterns – that is, patterns of behaviour for the entire class and for specific students. It's about reading the room and the individuals within the room. It's also about spotting those mini behaviours that can become mini misbehaviours and intervening quickly. In short, the withit teacher knows what's going on and demonstrates that awareness by actively managing the class.

The opposite of withitness is withoutitness: the teacher doesn't know what the students are doing or what they might do in different situations. This puts them on the behaviour management back foot. Consequently, they tend to be reactive rather than proactive, responding to misbehaviour in the moment rather than taking a preventative or strategic approach. Not only that, they are often slow to intervene. Hence, the misbehaviour gets worse, making it even harder to deal with.

Tip 5. Follow the Policy

Every school has a behaviour policy (it's a legal requirement) and you must know yours in detail. It will specify the school rules, detail the use of warnings and sanctions and (probably) describe the responsibilities of designated staff, such as those on call. It may also contain behaviour management advice.

When you know the policy in detail, you will be able to use it with confidence. But if you are shaky about its content, unsure about its processes and procedures, then you'll begin to doubt yourself. You might start thinking, "Well, maybe the student's right. Maybe it's not a C3, maybe it is a C2", and that lack of certainty will lead to a lack of confidence, and from there a lack of effectiveness.

Behaviour management is a team sport. Every teacher needs to be pulling in the same direction and doing things in the same way, and the behaviour policy is the school's way of achieving that end. If you follow it, everyone wins – that's you, your colleagues and the students. But if you don't follow it, if you pick and choose the bits you want and discount the bits you don't, you'll weaken the document, undermine your colleagues and make the process of teaching and learning that much harder.

The policy will take less than an hour to read, probably a lot less, and it's time well spent. So read it, learn it and follow it.

One Other Thing ...

I have a task for you. Go through each of the five super tips again and assess how well you currently meet them. Give yourself a score out of ten, with ten equalling 'fully'. Be blisteringly honest – only you will know the score so there's no one you need to impress. Next, read the rest of the book and keep those numbers in mind as you do. It will help to focus your thinking.

Note

1   Kounin, J. S. (1970). *Discipline and Group Management in Classrooms*. New York: Holt, Rinehart and Winston.

2 Relationship Rules

The teacher-student relationship influences all aspects of classroom behaviour. When it's effective, the students are more likely to accept your expectations, follow your instructions and work for your affirmation and praise. But when it's ineffective, student behaviour worsens, teaching becomes more difficult and learning is negatively impacted. Hence, it's a relationship you need to get right and this chapter will show you how.

Tip 6. Nice Boss

You need these two sets of qualities:

- Pleasant and polite.
- Confident and assertive.

Being pleasant and polite is the decent way to behave – and that's justification enough for the pairing. That said, they're also pragmatically helpful, not least in smoothing interactions, keeping relationships in good working order and making you a likeable person (or, at least, not an unlikeable one).

But, on their own, they're not enough. If being pleasant and polite is all you are, then some students will take advantage and behave in ways they know they shouldn't. Some might even try to walk all over you. So, besides being pleasant and polite, you've also got to be confident and assertive. You must be the boss and take charge of student behaviour.

Most tips in this book relate to the 'boss' bit of 'nice boss'. That's simply because being nice is easier than being the boss. But you must be both in about equal measure. When you are the boss (confident and assertive), you make the classroom a safe place, and when you are nice (pleasant and polite), you become a safe teacher in that safe place. The students don't have to worry about you or their peers because you've taken control of both concerns. Hence, all their focus can be on their learning.

Tip 7. Calm and Collected

You must stay calm and collected when misbehaviour happens – that is, you must be able to control your **Fight-or-Flight Response** (Chapter 13), your inbuilt and automatic way of dealing with perceived threats. When you are calm and collected, you'll be more likely to make good decisions and – even more importantly – less likely to make poor ones.

Most self-control strategies use a form of self-talk, either a reframing device or a mental script. Let's go through both.

Reframe

When you reframe a situation, you reconceptualise it in a more helpful way. Consider these two different ways of thinking about the same student behaviour:

> *This boy is always doing his best to wind me up!*
>
> *This is an opportunity to help the student develop self-control.*

Brilliant Behaviour in 60 Seconds or Less

Both frames might be accurate ways of describing the situation, but it is only the second one that helps you stay in control of your thoughts and behaviour, and thus gives the possibility of a successful outcome. Make sure you avoid emotional language and absolutes (e.g. 'wind me up' and 'always').

Mental Script

A mental script is a pre-prepared thought or series of thoughts. It is used to deal with situations that are a common problem for the teacher. For example:

> *I am scared but I'm not going to give into fear. Instead, I will calmly tell the student that their behaviour is inappropriate, and that I will speak to them at the end of the lesson.*

This example can also work as a template for any negative emotion. All you do is swap out the words 'scared' and 'fear' with whatever the emotion might be.

You can also use a mental script to deal with thoughts that arise after the event. For example:

> *In 24 hours' time I will not give this situation any thought whatsoever, so there's no need to be bothered by it now.*

Another form of mental script is an If-Then. It's another pre-prepared thought, but it's structured as a contingency. If the 'if' happens, then you do the 'then'. For example:

- *If I feel scared, then I will tell myself to be brave and professional.*
- *If I feel angry, then I will tell myself to be calm and professional.*
- *If I feel vengeful, then I will walk away and only speak to the student when I am certain I can control my response.*

The more you remind yourself of the If-Then, the more it becomes neurologically encoded. Hence, the more it becomes an automatic thought. For more on If-Thens, see Tip 95 of the same name.

Tip 8. Boringly Predictable

When you are boringly predictable, your students will know where they stand with you. They'll understand your expectations and be able to work to those expectations. They'll understand your boundaries and be able to keep within those boundaries. They'll understand your way of doing things and be able to do things your way. In short, they will understand how you function as a teacher and that will give them reassuring stability.

But if you're inconsistent, if you are erratic and changeable, you'll become a barrier to learning. At best, you'll lose your students' respect; at worst, you'll fill them with anxiety as they try to second guess which 'you' they're going to get.

So, be the same person on Monday morning, Friday afternoon and all points in between. Also, be the same person with every one of your students.

Tip 9. Show an Interest

Your students are not just learners in your lessons, but they're also individuals with lives outside the classroom and school, and it's good to show an interest in those lives.

You don't need to be nosey or ask lots of questions. All you have to do is simply clock snippets of information that come to the surface over time and then use that information when opportunities arise. For instance, if you know that a student's football team did well at the weekend, mention the result. If you saw a student in the school play, say something positive about their performance. If you know a student's cat has gone missing, ask if it's been found.

You can also show an interest by drawing on your students' hobbies, skills and knowledge. Most students like the opportunity to be an expert in the classroom, and even those that say they don't, secretly, most of them do too. Likewise, if a student made an interesting and relevant observation in a previous lesson, refer to it in the current one.

These are small things, yet they communicate something powerful. They tell the student that they are significant and worthy of your interest and thought. And that, in turn, can positively affect the quality of the teacher-student relationship. Simply put, we like people who take an interest in us, so take an interest.

Tip 10. Clean Slate

Do not let previous misbehaviour negatively influence how you treat the student in the current lesson. Instead, be warm and welcoming and make sure they get the same opportunities to contribute as all other students. In other words, wipe the slate clean every lesson.

This does not mean, however, that you should forget about the previous misbehaviour. It is entirely appropriate to be warm, welcoming and inclusive *and* to remind the student of your behaviour expectations. In fact, reminding is something you should do at the start of the very next lesson. When you take this dual approach – clean slate plus clear expectations – you set the student up for success.

One Other Thing ...

When I visit schools and deliver Continuing Professional Development, I often ask teachers about their best teacher when they were children. I get lots of lovely responses, with these being the most common:

- Firm but fair.
- Strict.
- A good person.

Relationship Rules

- Controlled the room.
- Kind.
- Knew where you stood.
- Approachable.
- Warm.
- Boundaried.
- Made it safe.

These responses all point to the same idea: their best teacher was a **Nice Boss** (Tip 6), a decent person who took charge of the classroom and made it a safe and calm place for learning. So aim for that relationship style – not only is it the most effective way to be, but it's also what your students prefer, which makes it a win-win.

3 Presence and Clarity

Presence and clarity work together. When you have the former, the students are more likely to give you their full attention; and when you have the latter, they are more likely to understand what you're saying. Combined, the students are more likely to behave as you want them to behave. This close connection is why presence and clarity are considered in the same chapter.

Tip 11. Positioning and Posture

Take a central and commanding position when you address the class. Stand square on and take up space. Don't fidget or pace because it's distracting and conveys nervousness. Own the space by being still and self-contained. When you use positioning and posture in this way, you present as confident and in charge.

Tip 12. Eye Contact

Insist that all students are looking at you when you address the class. Have a set phrase to prompt their attention, such as 'eyes on me' or 'track me'. At the same time, scan the students to increase their compliance. Our innate setting is to look at people when they are speaking to us, to the point that it feels rude not to (at least,

Presence and Clarity

that's the case for most people), so let your gaze settle on a few random and not-so-random students.

Getting eye contact from students has three benefits. First, the students pick up on your non-verbal communication and that helps clarity and comprehension. Second, you come across as a confident teacher and that enhances presence. Third, the students are less likely to be distracted or cause distractions and that maintains focus.

Tip 13. Exaggerated Non-Verbals

Non-verbal communication includes gestures, facial expressions, physical movement, delivery pauses, body posture and eye contact. To be clear and compelling, these elements must be exaggerated. Subtle non-verbals are easily missed and misunderstood, so think of yourself as an actor playing to the cheap seats at the back of the theatre. That's the level of exaggeration you're after. We'll return to this tip when we look at **Pull a Face** (Tip 65) and **Give a Gesture** (Tip 66).

Tip 14. Confident Voice

Speak with the expectation that what you are saying will be listened to. Take out any nervousness, hesitancy or apologetic tone. Also, don't rush. When you rush, you tell your students that what you're saying isn't important because if it was important you wouldn't rush. Instead, use a deliberate and crisp delivery. Devices such as dramatic pauses, keyword emphasis and repetition – and indeed repetition (and repetition) – can help to highlight key content. Another useful device is the next tip, **Big Quiet**.

Tip 15. Big Quiet

This is where you reduce your spoken volume but exaggerate your non-verbal delivery. Specifically, you speak just above a whisper while amplifying your body language, particularly gestures and facial expressions. This 'big quiet' combination catches the students' interest and prompts silent attention. In effect, you're telling your students that what you're saying is so fantastically fascinating that they really shouldn't miss a single word.

The process works as a chain reaction. Initially, a small group of students will quieten down and listen to you. Their attentiveness, in turn, prompts a second wave of students to do the same. Very soon, silent attention has spread across the classroom. You now have the students where you want them.

Big Quiet is also a useful transitioning device. You grab the students' attention (see **Attention Grabbers**, Chapter 7), immediately shift into Big Quiet and deliver the instruction, and then crisply move on to the next part of the lesson.

Tip 16. Casual Confidence

Most discussions about presence focus on its formal classroom elements, and we've done the same in this chapter. But you also need presence for less formal interactions, such as exploring an idea with students or having a class discussion. At those times, you need to exude casual confidence.

The core elements of presence stay the same. You still take up space, face the students square on and get eye contact, but you are more relaxed in how you do those things. You might lean against the side of your desk or perhaps even perch on top of it. Your body language will be more open and the way you speak more conversational. You'll probably smile and nod more, too. Low-key humour might also feature. Yet, you are still very much the boss, orchestrating contributions and managing behaviour. In fact, it is the casualness of your approach together with an abundance of confidence that tells the students that you are very much the person in charge.

Tip 17. Concise and Precise

Use the fewest words possible and be exact in your word choice. Avoid jargon and technical words unless you've taught those words. Plain English is best. Do not let your word choice be a barrier to understanding.

Tip 18. Front-Load the 'How'

Tell students how to follow an instruction before you tell them what to do. For example:

- *You are going to answer some workbook questions in silence …* [then tell them which questions]
- *You will be working in your set pairs using your quiet voice …* [then tell them the task]
- *Put up your hands – no calling out! – if you can answer this question …* [then ask the question]

Do it the other way round and the students won't pay attention to the 'how', which means they'll be less likely to do things the way you want them done.

Tip 19. Take Small Steps

If the instruction or explanation has any degree of complexity or difficulty, only give one item of information at a time. If it's a simple communication, then you can give up to three items of information, but not more than that. Three will keep you on the safe side of cognitive overload.

Tip 20. Describe and Demonstrate

Describe what you're doing while you're doing it. Whether it's how to put the Lego neatly away, safely collect a Bunsen burner or politely contribute to a class discussion, when you describe and demonstrate, you get two routes into your students' working memory. Hence, the students are clearer about what to do.

Tip 21. Display Key Information

Display the key information visually and then explain that information. Flow diagrams, numbered lists and bullet points work very well. Here, for instance, is a bullet point list instructing students how to use mini-whiteboards (MWB):

- Write your answer on the MWB.
- Turn the MWB over so it is face down.
- Put the MWB pen down.
- Don't look at any anyone else's answer.
- On my cue, show me your answer.

The other benefit of displayed information is that it acts as an ongoing reminder of what to do.

Tip 22. Just-in-Time Reminding

This is where you remind students of the required behaviour (your rules, routines, expectations or instructions) just before it needs to be done. For example:

- *In a moment, you will be working independently. Remember, that means total focus and silent working.*
- *When you enter the classroom, sit according to the seating plan.*
- *We will be going to the school library. You'll be walking in your set pairs. No talking. Everyone needs to keep up with the pair in front.*

Presence and Clarity

Just-in-Time Reminding proactively promotes the behaviour you want by putting it at the forefront of your students' thinking. Reminding after the event isn't really reminding at all, but a type of feedback. It's fine as feedback, but it has little usefulness as a reminder. As a rule, proactive beats reactive.

Tip 23. Recap Main Points

Recapping reminds students of the key points you've just made. If it comes just before a task or activity, then it's also a form of **Just-in-Time Reminding** (previous tip). Try to limit the key points to three items of information so cognitive load (the amount of information being processed) isn't an issue. If it's more than three items, use **Display Key Information** (Tip 21) to help carry the load. You can also use **Check for Understanding** (next tip) for reinforcement.

Tip 24. Check for Understanding

Always check for understanding if it's a complex instruction or an important one. Here's why:

- It assesses understanding.
- It clarifies understanding.
- It increases retention.
- It highlights the importance of the instruction.
- It tells students what to do just at the point they need to know it.

The most common way to check for understanding is through random sampling, that is, getting one or two students to explain in their own words what you've just said. It's helpful to choose a student who doesn't always pay as much attention as they might. You can also use the 'everybody votes' and 'mini-whiteboard' approaches from **Peak Participation** (Tip 30) to check for whole-class understanding.

Tip 25. Narrate Compliance

This is where you publicly describe the behaviour of the students who are behaving appropriately. For example:

- *This group is silent and tracking me. As is this group. That's how we do things in this classroom.*
- *James is sitting with his book open, ready to learn. As is Chaya, as is Anita, as is Michael.*
- *The majority of you have already picked up your pens and are ready to start writing.*

Narrate Compliance has three benefits. First, it has perfect timing. You're reminding the students at the precise moment they need to know. Second, it leverages social proof and thus prompts students to align their behaviour to those around them. Third, it helps to normalise appropriate behaviour so that it becomes a fixed feature of your classroom culture.

This third benefit is the most important of all. However, for normalisation to happen, you've got to narrate compliance frequently and throughout the year. A common mistake is to stop after a couple of lessons. Hence, the normalising effect doesn't take hold. For more on social proof and normalisation, see **Introduction: Conformity**.

One Other Thing ...

Presence and clarity also reduce wriggle room. When you've insisted that students give you their full attention and you've been clear in what you've said, it makes it very difficult for students to claim that they don't know what to do. Hence, compliance increases.

4 The Fundamentals

This chapter considers the day-to-day conditions and approaches that are necessary for brilliant student behaviour. As with so many aspects of behaviour management, it is the consistent application of the fundamentals that leads to success.

Tip 26. Classroom Layout

The best default is 'rows and columns' with students sitting in pairs. First, all students are facing you, which means it's more likely that they'll understand what you're telling or showing them. Second, it's easier to move around the classroom to support, nudge or correct the students as necessary. Third, it facilitates paired work, and paired work is a form of **Peak Participation** (Tip 30). The more students you have working, the more you have behaving and learning. Lastly, it's versatile. If you want students to work in a group of four, the pair in front simply turns around and works with the pair behind. And when the work's done, they turn back again and give you their silent attention.

Why not use table groups as your default layout? Because human beings are social animals and working in groups encourages that social nature. Consequently, you get a lot more chatting and a lot less focus. Also, by design, some students will have their backs to you, meaning they'll miss your non-verbal communication, such as gestures, body posture, positioning and eye contact. You can, of course, tell them to turn around and face you, but all of that takes time, and lost time equates to lost learning. Lastly, table groups (and all group working) makes something called **Social Loafing** (Chapter 13) much more likely. Simply put, the students sit back and let others do the work.

Tip 27. Seating Plan

Do not allow students to decide where to sit. Do that and you are likely to have a challenging year ahead. Instead, sit students according to the register and, if you are co-educational, sit girls next to boys. These measures will reduce chatting.

Make sure, too, that you factor in relationships that are likely to cause behavioural issues (e.g. enemies or, worse, friends). If you don't know the students, ask the form tutor or head of year if there are any issues you need to know about. For more on this, see **Find Out** (Tip 94).

It's also helpful to sit less hardworking students next to more hardworking ones. The less hardworking students tend to work harder, rather than the other way round. Similarly, sit less attentive students behind attentive ones. When those less attentive students see others attending to you, they'll be more likely to do the same.

At the start of every term and half term, display your seating plan so that students can take their seats quickly and without fuss. Keep it displayed for a few lessons to embed this requirement and reduce wriggle room.

Also, make sure you stick to your seating plan throughout the year. If you must change it, change it to serve teaching and learning

The Fundamentals

needs, but don't change it because of friendship requests or as a bargaining chip for good behaviour. Once the students know you won't change, they'll stop asking.

One caveat: some teachers change their seating plans half-termly or termly. They do it to help classroom cohesion and to make sure that no single student has to sit next to a tricky student for the entire year. This is entirely reasonable. That said, this strategy is probably more helpful for teachers in primary schools or those that teach the core subjects in secondary schools. It's not so needed for teachers who see students less frequently.

The other great thing about a seating plan is that it helps you learn your students' names – which is the next tip.

Tip 28. Know Names

Make it a priority to learn your students' names as soon as possible (that's all of your students, not just the noisier ones), and then use those names frequently. It's respectful, inclusive and contributes to classroom cohesion.

Using a student's name also makes the correction of student misbehaviour more effective:

- *Peter, four on the floor and eyes on me.*
- *Greg, eyes and ears.*
- *Bianca, close your book and put your pen down.*

If you ever get a name wrong, apologise and make sure you don't get it wrong a second time. In fact, pledge to yourself that you won't and then actively test yourself to make sure you never do.

Knowing your students' names is also a prerequisite for the next tip, **Cold Call/No Opt Out**.

Tip 29. Cold Call/No Opt Out

Cold Call and No Opt Out are two closely related strategies promoted by Doug Lemov in his wonderful book *Teach Like a Champion*. Let's go through each in turn.

Cold Call

This is a no-hands-up approach to asking questions. The teacher asks a question, inserts some thinking time and then chooses a student to answer. For example:

> What did Lady Macbeth mean when she said 'look like the innocent flower but be the serpent under it'? [insert thinking time]. Becky?

Make sure the student's name goes at the end of the Cold Call, not the beginning. Do it the other way around and you invite the rest of the class to zone out.

No Opt Out

Do not allow a student to opt out from answering. If the student doesn't know the answer, do one of the following:

- The student discusses the question with their partner (the rest of the class do the same), and then you ask the student again. Ten or so seconds is often enough.
- You or a student gives a single clue.
- You or a student gives the answer and the student repeats that answer.

Later in the lesson, ask the student the same question again.

Cold Call/No Opt Out increases student attention by increasing student accountability. Your students don't know who you are going to pick, but they know that if you pick them, they'll have to answer.

Tip 30. Peak Participation

Ensure that all tasks, activities and interactions get peak participation from your students, that is, every student is stretched and engaged by the work. The previous tip, **Cold Call/No Opt Out** is helpful for this, as are the following approaches:

- Independent work.
- Think-pair-share.
- Mini-whiteboards.
- Everybody votes.
- Say it again.

Independent Work

As a rule of thumb, independent and silent working is the summit of peak participation. As such, it should feature every lesson, and that can mean multiple times, too.

Think-Pair-Share

All paired work gives high participation rates, but the structure of think-pair-share is particularly helpful because it adds independent thinking (the 'think' bit) and accountability (the 'share' bit). It works like this: you ask a question; you give the students thinking time; they discuss their thoughts in pairs; you then choose a student to share their answer with the class.

Brilliant Behaviour in 60 Seconds or Less

Mini-Whiteboards

Mini-whiteboards are useful for both simple and complex answers. To stop copying, get students to place them face down until you call for them to be shown. For more on mini-whiteboards, see **Display Key Information** (Tip 21).

Everybody Votes

You ask the class a question, provide thinking time, and then, to stop any copying, get all the students to answer as one. The vote can be a show of hands, fingers to indicate multiple-choice responses, raised and lowered thumbs or an answer on a mini-whiteboard.

Say It Again

You get a student to repeat the answer that was just given. You can also use a chain of 'say it agains' with students immediately following on from one another – What did he just say? What did she just say? What did Jamie just say? What did Davina just say? Everyone together, what did Kim just say?

Tip 31. Visible Scan

Scan the students and make it obvious that you are scanning them. You'll have a better idea of what's going on, and, just as importantly, the students will know that you do so the likelihood of misbehaviour reduces.

There are four scanning techniques:

- Delivery scan.
- One-minute scan.
- Default scan.
- Pivot and check.

The Fundamentals

Delivery Scan

This is what you do when you are addressing the class. You stand front and centre and scan the entire room as you speak, letting your gaze settle momentarily on random (and not so random) students. Doing this prompts eye contact and attentiveness, while at the same time demonstrating your confidence.

One-Minute Scan

There's a lag period between the start of an activity and when that activity grabs the students. It's around 20–30 seconds but can be as much as a minute – hence, you need to do a one-minute scan. You do that by standing in a central position and making it obvious that you're scanning. You might step to the left and scan. You might crane your neck to the right and scan. You might even go on tippy-toes and scan. By making it obvious, you're letting the students know that they're being observed and that prompts them to focus on their work.

If a student hasn't started working, try to deal with it non-verbally so you don't distract the rest of the class. A gesture to pick up their pen works well, as does walking towards the student while looking at them. Adding a thumbs up confirms that you are now happy with their behaviour.

When you are satisfied that all of your students are working and engaged, you can cautiously move on to other things, such as taking a quiet question or checking work. Alternatively, you can keep on scanning – aka do a default scan.

Default Scan

It's called a default scan because this is the scan you should default to when the students are working. You can scan from the front of the classroom (that's the spot with the most presence), or you can move to one of the front corners. To save your legs but keep some height, you can perch on a stool or the side of your desk (as suggested by Doug Lemov in *Teach Like a Champion*). It is useful if you scan from the same location because then the students will associate that place with being observed.

Pivot and Check

This is what you do when you have your back to the students, for instance, when writing on the whiteboard, walking around the classroom or working with a small group of students. Simply put, you turn around to see what's going on behind you. Do it frequently and irregularly so the students have the idea that they might be observed at any moment.

Tip 32. Start Line

Make the start of an activity like the start of a race. In other words, inject urgency and get all the students working at exactly the same moment. A crisp phrase like this works well:

> Pens at the ready ... begin!

'Pens at the ready' is the primer. It primes the students for the type of activity, in this case writing. This equates to the race official calling out 'on your marks'.

After the primer, you need to pause (...). One or two seconds is enough. The pause gives the students a moment to get ready, to literally pick up their pen and be ready to write. It also creates anticipation for the start of the activity. To continue the sprint analogy, the pause equates to 'get set'.

The students are now on the start line waiting for the starting pistol to fire. You do that by saying the word 'begin'. You must say it with emphasis: go for crisp and definite. You can also add in a gesture for extra emphasis, such as your hand or index finger making a

The Fundamentals

chopping motion. Doing this while looking at your watch adds even more impetus to begin.

Here are a few more examples:

- *Brains at the ready ... think!*
- *Ideas at the ready ... share!*
- *Options at the ready ... list!*

Use Start Line in combination with the next tip, **Deadline**.

Tip 33. Deadline

Always set a fixed amount of time for a task to be completed. The tighter the deadline, the greater the pressure. If there's no deadline, there's no pressure – consequently, the students can take a leisurely approach, with time to chat, daydream or doodle. They might even be tempted to take a sneaky look at their phones.

Now, actually, the deadline doesn't have to be fixed, it only matters that the students *think* it's fixed. If you go over by a little and the students don't notice, then it's not a problem. That's why the classroom clock should be on the back wall: it's for you, not the students.

Also, use an irregular amount of time. So not a deadline of two, five or ten minutes, which sounds like you are being approximate, but, say, two minutes twenty, four minutes forty or nine minutes. It makes the deadline sound definite.

As the deadline approaches, use those two little words loved by shops and advertisers: 'just' and 'only'. These words have a minimising effect, making the remaining time seem less than it is. You can see this effect in these paired examples:

- *Ninety seconds left/Just ninety seconds left.*
- *Fifty seconds remaining/Only fifty seconds remaining.*

Brilliant Behaviour in 60 Seconds or Less

When deciding the duration of an activity, be guided by this principle: too little time is better than too much time. Too much time leads to off-task behaviour, while too little time, though not ideal, at least keeps the pressure in place.

Also, don't forget that students can get lots of work done in a short space of time – all they need is effort and focus which, happily, are what they get when you set a short deadline. In other words, the short deadline might not be that short after all.

Use Deadline in combination with the previous tip, **Start Line**.

Tip 34. Prised Praise Is Prized

Sorry for the tongue twister, but here's the point: praise that is difficult for the students to achieve (i.e. they have to 'prise' it out of you) is the praise they really prize.

When you praise too easily or frequently, you devalue the praise and make it not worth working for. You also lower the bar of your expectations. You tell your students that everyday behaviour is worthy of extra and special recognition when it's not. What's worthy of extra and special recognition is extra and special behaviour. Worse, to maintain the same level of effort and compliance, you're forced into giving even more praise. In effect, you end up running faster just to stand still.

Make sure, too, that you avoid using glowing adjectives such as wonderful, fantastic, brilliant, etc. Instead, neutrally state what they did and what you liked about it:

- *You opened the door. That was respectful.*
- *You put up your hand and waited in silence. Patience is what we do in this classroom.*
- *I liked the way you politely asked that question.*

The Fundamentals

One caveat: at the beginning of the academic year, praise students for following your rules, routines and expectations. This will reinforce those requirements. Once embedded, though, stop praising and instead **Narrate Compliance** (Tip 25), that is, describe the behaviour of the students who are behaving appropriately.

Tip 35. Thank in Advance

Thank students for following your instructions before they've actually done so. For example:

- *Jack, put your gum in the bin, thank you.*
- *Lyra, thank you for being quiet while I read the story.*
- *Class, pens down, thank you.*

This technique assumes compliance. After all, if you didn't think they were going to do it, why would you thank them?

Also, don't say 'please'. It sounds like you are pleading. Just say 'thank you' instead.

One Other Thing ...

There is nothing magical, mysterious or complex in this chapter. The tips are simple to understand and easy to do (if not very easy to do). The trick, though, is that you must apply them consistently – that's lesson after lesson, day after day. When you maintain this consistent approach, you normalise brilliant student behaviour and so create the conditions for excellent learning over the long term.

5 Embed Routines

When you embed routines into your classroom culture, everyone wins. Teaching and learning gets easier, the students work harder and with greater focus, and, as consequence, progress is optimised. But when routines are not embedded, you get the opposite of all of those things – and a lot more misbehaviour besides. Chapter 6, the next chapter, will look at several key routines, but for now the focus is on how to fix those routines in place. After all, a routine is only a routine when it's routine followed.

Tip 36. Design Your Routines

Your classroom will have routines whether you like it or not. If you leave those routines to chance or let them be shaped by student choices, at best they'll be inefficient and at worse counterproductive. Therefore, you (or other adults in the school) must design the routines.

The best routines have three features:

- An efficient structure.
- A vivid cue.
- Stable steps.

Embed Routines

An efficient structure makes the routine easier to learn and remember. A vivid cue ensures it happens when it should. And stable steps means that it's always done in the same way. Make sure you keep these features in mind when you design your routines.

Tip 37. Teach Your Routines

Routines need to be explicitly taught. Never assume the students will simply know what to do or how to behave. Some might, but others won't. And even those who do know, even they won't know *exactly* how you want things done. So teach them. Here's how:

- Give a rationale.
- Explain in detail.
- Check for understanding.
- Guide practice.
- Perform perfection.

Give a Rationale

A rationale increases student buy-in. It might not get buy-in from all of students, but it will get it from some and probably most and that leverages social proof (see **Introduction: Conformity**).

All routines have their own specific rationale, but you can also use one or more of the following: (1) increased teaching time, (2) increased learning time, (3) fewer distractions and (4) a safer classroom. Whatever the rationale might be, give it.

Explain in Detail

Explain each sequential step in nitpicky detail. Use **Describe and Demonstrate** (Tip 20) and **Display Key Information** (Tip 21) for extra clarity – that is, explain what you are doing as you do it and list the sequential steps on the whiteboard. These two different types of explanation give two different routes into your students' working memory (i.e. the brain's storage area for temporary information) and that helps comprehension.

Check for Understanding

The most common way to do this is through random sampling:

> Marilyn, what's the first step in the routine? Chaya, what's the second step? Isaac, can you be talking while this routine is going on or it is done in silence? Yep, you're right. The routine is done in silence.

Guide Practice

Get the students to practise the routine and then give them detailed feedback. Use a whole-class or small group approach (i.e. all the students practise or some of them do and the rest observe). Either way, give feedback that's nitpicky – it will convey your high expectations.

Perform Perfection

The entire class performs the routine perfectly. If they don't achieve perfection, give more detailed feedback and get them to have another go.

Tip 38. Insist and Persist

Getting routines embedded into your classroom culture can sometimes be difficult, particularly if you've inherited the class partway through the year. But you mustn't give up. If you do, you'll miss out on the benefits that routines bring, that is, those efficient and fuss-free behaviours that make teaching and learning a smooth and productive experience.

Embed Routines

So, insist and persist. And, if need be, insist and persist some more, and keep on insisting and persisting until you overcome all resistance. It's worth the effort.

Tip 39. Stick to Your Routines

When a routine is routinely followed, it takes on the power of habit – that is, it happens unthinkingly and without question. But when it's not followed as it should be followed, when steps are missed or it's done in a haphazard way, the routine falls apart. Simply put, when there's no consistency, there's no habit.

Sometimes, of course, for reasons beyond your control, a routine does get broken. If this happens once, it's not good but it's not a disaster. As long as it's followed correctly the next time, there won't be any long-term damage.

But if the routine is not followed *twice in succession*, then that's much more problematic. Unfortunately, a new pattern of behaviour has begun and it's on the verge of becoming fixed. Hence, you'll have to take remedial action, that is, you'll need to remind the students of the sequential steps in detail, check for understanding and then observe them closely as the routine is carried out. It might also be useful to **Narrate Compliance** (Tip 25), or at the very least make the act of observing really obvious.

If a routine is not followed three *times in succession*, then almost certainly it's no longer a routine. There might be a faint memory, but there isn't a firm pattern. Your only option now is to reteach the routine from scratch (Tip 37).

Tip 40. Remind and Revisit

Frequently remind the students of the sequential steps within your routines. Use a combination of **Just-in-Time Reminding** (Tip 22)

Brilliant Behaviour in 60 Seconds or Less

and **Narrate Compliance** (Tip 25). The frequency can reduce over the year, but you should never stop reminding entirely.

Also, make sure you revisit your routines more fully when there's been a break in the academic year (Christmas, Easter, half-term, etc.). Go through the 'why, when and how' of your routines, that is, explain why they are in place, when they should happen and how they should be followed. Then get the students to practise the routines – and do this even if they are already perfect. It elevates the importance of your routines while at the same time reducing wriggle room.

One Other Thing …

If you regularly get misbehaviour at the same point in a lesson, then almost certainly a routine is missing. So create a routine to fit that gap. If you think you do have a routine in place, then it's either poorly designed or not firmly embedded – which, in effect, means the same thing as 'missing'. In that case, you will need to reteach the routine.

6 Key Routines

Different teachers will have different key routines, reflecting what they teach, the age of their students and their own preferences. While it's not possible to give an exhaustive list, the routines that follow are appropriate for most teachers in most settings. Use them as written or as starting points for designing your own routines.

Tip 41. Meet, Greet and Seat

Meet and greet your students at the classroom door. Be warm and welcoming, but also take charge and manage their behaviour. In other words, use your **Nice Boss** (Tip 6) qualities. If possible, stand so you can look down the corridor and into the classroom from the same spot. If it's practical to line the students up in the corridor, do so and let them enter the classroom one at a time, insisting on silence as they do. Use the doorway threshold as the cue for silence – it's vivid and stable and reinforces the boundary between corridor behaviour and classroom expectations.

Hold back any student who is not ready to enter (e.g. overexcited, has a uniform issue, talking, etc.). This is also the time to do a **Commitment Remind** (Tip 89), that is, to remind students of any commitment they've made to change their behaviour.

Brilliant Behaviour in 60 Seconds or Less

Make sure you have routines for coats and bags. Aim for neat, tidy and safe.

Make sure, too, that you have a routine for the distribution of exercise books. Go for quick, efficient and fuss-free. For more on this, see **Slick Transitions** (Tip 44) and **Distribute Resources** (Tip 45).

Ensure students sit according to your **Seating Plan** (Tip 27), and once seated, they start working straightaway – a good way to do that is with the next tip, **Do Now**.

Tip 42. Do Now

This tip draws heavily from Doug Lemov's excellent *Teach Like a Champion*.

A Do Now is a five-minute activity that students complete at the start of the lesson. It gets the students working immediately and sets a productive tone. It also gives you an opportunity to take the register, sort out any unforeseen issues and settle yourself.

An effective Do Now is a quiz called 'sevens'. You display seven questions on the whiteboard. Questions one, two and three link to the previous lesson, while questions four to seven loop back to previous weeks and months. You can also use one of the questions as a link to the lesson you are about to teach. 'Sevens' is a form of spaced retrieval. In other words, it combines spaced practice with retrieval practice and as such is one of the best ways there is to encode learning into long-term memory.

Always display the Do Now in the same place (e.g. the interactive whiteboard). Make sure it's easy to understand and relatively easy to do. You are not trying to stretch the students, but to help them encode previous learning. The work should be done independently and in silence. Keep resources simple, too. A pen and an exercise book are enough.

Key Routines

Finish with a rapid review of the answers. Do this to stop faulty methodology and incorrect information being retained. If your students are confused, make a note to reteach in a future lesson or even later in the current lesson, but not during the Do Now. Remember, it's a five-minute activity and you must stay close to that time. Finally, transition crisply to the next part of the lesson.

Tip 43. Late to Lesson

You need a routine for when a student is late to lesson. Here's one that works:

- The student enters the classroom in silence.
- The student waits by the classroom door until acknowledged by you.
- Once acknowledged, the student takes their seat.
- They do not talk to any other student.
- If the student doesn't understand the work, they put up their hand and wait for your help.

Regarding the last bullet point, another option is to allow the student next to them to whisper what to do.

If you don't know why the student is late, wait until the class is engaged in work and then go and find out. Don't publicly ask because it's distracting and the answer might be personal.

Tip 44. Slick Transitions

Make transitions as slick as possible. Whether it's between activities, exercises, instructions, demonstrations or explanations, go for crisp, efficient and fuss-free.

Slick transitions have three important benefits. First, they optimise lesson time. Transitions are deadtime, so the slicker they are, the more time there is for learning. Second, they reduce the opportunity for misbehaviour. Simply put, the students don't have time to misbehave because they're already onto the next task. Third, they communicate a very important message, namely, that your classroom is a place where working hard is the expectation.

Slick Transitions links to the next tip, **Distribute Resources.**

Tip 45. Distribute Resources

There are five common ways to distribute resources:

1. The students collect the resources.
2. Student helpers hand out the resources.
3. You use the 'take one and pass it on' approach.
4. You hand out resources when the students are working.
5. You hand out resources between activities.

All approaches can work well when established as routines. That said, the first is potentially the most problematic so requires the tightest oversight, including a staggered collection of the resources. The second is a good compromise between speed and control. Your student helpers are doing the work, which frees you up to supervise. The third can be lightning quick when the students are well drilled. Also, there's something unifying and cohesive about working together as an efficient team. The fourth is the fastest (the resources are in front of the students and ready to be used), but there is also a risk that you might distract the students from their current work.

The fifth approach, handing out resources between activities, is the slowest and gives the poorest control. The problem is that your attention is split between distribution and supervision when it should be fully on the latter. Also, unavoidably, you'll have your back to some of the students which is never a good thing. So, if you are going to take this approach, make sure your students know to be patient and silent, and that you frequently 'pivot and check' (Tip 31) to make sure they are. Lastly, don't give out instructions at the same time because it will impact your clarity and slow you down.

Tip 46. Get Teacher's Attention

Your students need a routine for getting your attention. It must include the elements of patience, politeness and productivity. Here's a routine that works:

- Students put up their hand and wait in silence.
- Once acknowledged, they get on with 'other work'.
- They continue working until you get to them.

The 'other work' can be the next question, a different part of the task, checking and editing what they've already done, or testing themselves on subject-specific spellings. The point is this: a student should never have the option of doing nothing or claiming that they have nothing to do.

Tip 47. Silent Working

Silent working is a win-win. It's a win for the students because it allows for uninterrupted concentration, and it's a win for you because it gives mental space and a chance to take stock of where you are in the lesson.

Be very careful not to distract students during silent working. So, for instance, when you are supporting a student or handing out resources, do so as silently and unobtrusively as possible. If you're even a little bit noisy, you'll break the spell of silence and that's when chatting starts.

Brilliant Behaviour in 60 Seconds or Less

Ideally, most (if not all) of your time should be spent doing a **Visible Scan** (Tip 31), specifically a 'default scan'. Its visibility will help prompt compliance, as will your modelling of stillness and silence.

Silent working is also a prerequisite for that phenomenon known as the flow state or the zone. It's a sort of 'super silent working' where the students direct their full attention to the task. Time seems to disappear and the work becomes fully engrossing and deeply pleasurable. Misbehaviour rarely happens, and even if it does, most students don't notice it, or if they do, don't engage with it.

You won't get a flow state every time with silent working, but you'll never get it without it. If you're aiming to create this phenomenon, go for a single, lengthy piece of work (i.e. longer than ten minutes) and set it in the stretch zone (i.e. not too easy and not too hard). Fragmented tasks such as students working through a series of quick questions, important though that work is, won't lead to the flow state.

There is no reason why silent learning (flow state or not) shouldn't feature in every single lesson, and multiple times at that.

Tip 48. Setting Homework

When setting homework, do the following:

- Insist on silent attention.
- Display the homework visually (e.g. bullet points or numbered lists).
- Explain the homework in detail (and don't rush).
- Check for understanding.
- Ensure students write the homework down.

Many schools use online homework platforms so there's no need for students to write the homework down. These systems can be really helpful, but if that's what your school does, then you'll need

Key Routines

to spend even more time explaining and checking. Things that are written down (particularly by hand rather than typed) are better understood and remembered.

Some teachers get students to start their homework in the lesson as a way of upping completion rates. There's no research on this (as far as I know), but it is supported by an interesting psychological quirk called the **Ovsiankina Effect** (Chapter 13). Simply put, we are motivated to complete tasks that we've started because not doing so causes psychological discomfort. Therefore, in theory, starting homework in the lesson, even if it is just for a minute or two, might be a useful strategy.

Tip 49. Exit Prep

Your exit preparation is everything you need to do after **Setting Homework** (previous tip) and before you **Dismiss the Students** (next tip). It's several routines in one and typically includes:

- Resources returned/collected.
- Work areas tidied.
- Litter picked up.
- Bags packed.
- Report cards checked and signed.

Use **Narrate Compliance** (Tip 25) to proactively manage the students. For example:

- *Andrew has tidied his work area and returned his equipment.*
- *Emily has returned the textbooks for her row.*
- *This group has packed their bags and are giving me their silent attention.*

At the start of the year, keep these 'sub-routines' separate until the students have demonstrated they can perform each one perfectly. If there's a dip in performance (e.g. students not doing a good enough job of tidying their work area), then separate them out again.

Make sure you give yourself plenty of time to do everything that needs to be done. Finishing a lesson early is better than finishing it rushed. If you rush, you'll forget to say or do something important. Also, when it comes to dismissing the students (next tip), it won't go as well as it should.

Tip 50. Dismiss the Students

This routine has three sequential parts:

- Silent attention.
- Stand behind desks.
- Staggered exit.

Silent Attention

Use an attention grabber (Chapter 7) to get the students' attention. **3-2-1 Countdown** (Tip 55) works particularly well. In other words, slowly count down from three to one with the expectation that when you get to 'one', all eyes will be on you.

Stand Behind Desks

Make the instruction concise and precise. For example:

> Class ... stand.

You can also add a gesture for extra clarity, such as raising your palms upwards. If a student talks, gesture them to be silent and sit back down. That student is now the last to leave. If you need to issue notices or reminders, this is the time to do it. If your school uses a bell, train the students to ignore it.

Key Routines

Staggered Exit

Dismiss the students one row, column or table group at a time, never all at once. Either take a central position or stand by the door and sprinkle a little positivity as they go: a nod, a smile, a thumbs up, a whispered comment of praise. But be cautious about starting a conversation – if you do, you'll likely prompt some students to talk amongst themselves. If a student wants to speak to you or you want to speak to a student, it's best to hold them back.

If you've ended the lesson early, have a simple, low-key (i.e. non-excitable) educational activity up your sleeve – or perhaps always end with such an activity, thus making it a part of the ending routine. Activities that incorporate spaced retrieval such as quizzes are ideal. If you do choose to use a quiz, make the questions relatively easy. End on success, not failure.

Tip 51. Absent Teacher

You need a routine for when you are away. Here's one that works:

- The students show unfailing courtesy to the cover teacher.
- They follow the cover teacher's instructions immediately.
- They follow set classroom routines (unless the cover teacher says differently).
- They sit according to the seating plan.

You could argue that the last bullet point is covered by the one before it. After all, sitting according to the seating plan is already a set routine. However, it's such an important requirement that it needs its own emphasis. If students don't sit where they should be sitting, behaviour will almost certainly be a problem. That's partly because the misbehaviour has already started (not sitting according to the seating plan is a form of misbehaviour) and partly because students are now sitting next to friends, and friends chat and have fun and make each other laugh and do silly things and egg each other on and – you get the idea.

If you know you're going to be away, let your students know too, and then display and go through your expectations again (as above). It acts as a reminder, underlines the importance of appropriate behaviour and reduces wriggle room.

Make it clear that though you are not expecting any behavioural problems, you will nevertheless check with the cover teacher to see how things went and will follow up on any misbehaviour should it be necessary. And make sure you stick to your word, too. It will help to prevent future problems.

Tip 52. Classroom Disturbance

If there's a (non-dangerous) disturbance in the classroom, by default, the students should ignore it and carry on working. That's the routine, and it's as simple as it is important.

Explain to the students that it doesn't matter what the disturbance is (e.g. a flickering lightbulb, a teacher coming in to borrow something, loud banging from building work outside, etc), they simply stay focused and carry on working. Explain too that if they need to do anything other than that, you'll tell them.

The most common form of classroom disturbance is misbehaviour, so this needs extra focus. Give some examples so the students are clear about what you mean, making sure you highlight chatting and playing the class clown. Make it clear that it's your job to deal with misbehaviour, not theirs, and that by not getting involved they are making it easier for you to manage the situation and for the misbehaving student to regain their self-control.

Key Routines

Give this caveat: if the student is acting dangerously, bullying someone or using or taking things that don't belong to them, you should be told straightaway.

Tip 53. Checklist

A checklist is a meta-routine that keeps all other routines in tip-top shape. Before every lesson, tick off the items in the checklist to make sure you've done them. Some will only need to be ticked once (e.g. date on the whiteboard), but others will need to be ticked each lesson. As the year progresses, adapt the checklist so it becomes an increasingly helpful document. Here's my checklist:

Activities planned.	Whiteboard eraser.
Transitions planned.	My resources ready.
Homework planned.	Student resources ready.
Date on whiteboard.	Exercise books ready.
Do Now displayed.	Textbooks counted.
Seating plan displayed.	Register open.
IT equipment checked.	Spare pens.
Internet resources open.	Spare lined paper.
Board markers working.	Classroom tidy.
Spare board markers.	Commitment Remind.

It's a long list but it only takes a minute to go through. Most items speak for themselves, though **Commitment Remind** (Tip 89) needs some explanation. Simply put, this is where you remind a student of a commitment they've made to change their behaviour. It's the final stage of a **Follow-Up Conversation** (Chapter 10).

Do not underestimate the usefulness of a checklist nor overestimate your ability to remember everything that needs to be done. You might think that you won't forget to do that important thing, but you will. So use a checklist.

One Other Thing ...

Routines have another benefit: they reduce the amount of information (i.e. the cognitive load) that students need to process. In other words, they don't have to think about where to sit, who to work with or how to get the teacher's attention, because there's a routine for those and other repeated events. Hence, all of their thinking and attention can go on their learning.

7 Attention Grabbers

You must be able to get your students' attention whenever you need it – that's instantly, completely and without fuss. The way to do that is with an attention grabber. It's another key routine and so could have featured in Chapter 6. However, because it's a prerequisite for optimal learning (without it you waste time), it deserves a chapter of its own.

Tip 54. Primer and Direction

The primer gets the students' attention, and the direction tells them what to do. For example:

Year 10s … eyes on me.

'Year 10s' is the primer and 'eyes on me' is the direction. Deliver the primer crisply and with energy, pause to give the students a moment to focus on you and then give the direction. Here are some more examples:

- *Hayley's group … you may leave in silence.*
- *Acorns … pens down.*
- *Year 4s … stand.*

Brilliant Behaviour in 60 Seconds or Less

You can also add a gesture for extra clarity and emphasis. For the examples above, respectively, that could be pointing to the door, putting down an imaginary pen or raising your palms upwards.

Tip 55. 3-2-1 Countdown

Use 3-2-1 Countdown when you want to give students a moment to finish a piece of work, such as a sentence they're writing or a point they're making to their work partner.

'Three' is the cue so you need to deliver it with volume and emphasis. You then slowly count down to 'one', dropping your volume as you do. Leave a second or two between numbers so the students have a chance to finish what they were doing. When you get to 'one', every student gives you their silent attention.

If you get to 'one' and there's still talking, look directly at the student (a quizzical look works well – Tip 65) and keep looking until the talking stops. Hold the look for a beat longer before crisply moving on. If the student talks over you again, use the same strategy but follow up with a stronger intervention such as **Public Anonymous** (Tip 69) or **Discreet Direction** (Tip 71).

Tip 56. Copy Me

Use this method when there is a lot of noise or if the students are dispersed over a large area, such as the playground, school hall or drama studio. You put a finger to your lips and raise your other hand in the air. The first student to notice you immediately stops talking and copies the same two actions. The next student to notice either you or the first student does the same – and so on. Very soon, silence sweeps across the learning space.

Attention Grabbers

Copy Me is a non-verbal form of communication so make sure it's exaggerated (see **Exaggerated Non-Verbals**, Tip 13). In other words, stand completely straight with your arm fully extended and your hand pointing directly upwards.

Tip 57. Call and Response

Call and Response works best with primary school students. You call out the first part of a set sentence, and the students instantly and collectively respond with the second half, and then immediately give you their silent attention. Here are some paired examples:

- *1, 2, 3, eyes on me/1, 2, eyes on you.*
- *Ready to listen/Ready to learn.*
- *Hocus Pocus/Time to focus.*
- *Macaroni cheese/Everybody freeze.*
- *Chicka, chicka/Boom, boom.*

Tip 58. Formality Switch

Formality Switch means switching the level of your formality to signal a change in activity or expectation. The switch is always from the informal to the formal and must be abrupt. If it's not those two things, it won't grab the students' attention.

Let's say you are perched on the edge of your desk facilitating a class discussion, as described in **Casual Confidence** (Tip 16), but now you want the entire class to move on to a different task. The Formality Switch could look like this: you abruptly stand up, hold yourself tall and straight, and crisply say 'class, eyes on me'. The combination of abruptness and formality instantly gets the students' attention. Hence, they are now ready to listen to the instruction.

Brilliant Behaviour in 60 Seconds or Less

One Other Thing ...

Attention grabbers not only help you manage the flow and direction of the lesson, but they also give a quick and easy way to regain control should things go awry. In that sense, they are both a reassuring safety net and a confidence boost. To be effective, though, as with all other routines, they need to be explicitly taught and frequently revisited. Make sure, too, that you embrace their performative nature and deliver them with gusto. Do that and the grabby bit will be even more grabby.

8 Strategic Corrections

The previous chapters have focused on the prevention of misbehaviour. Given that prevention is better than cure, that makes sense. But even with all the tips we've looked at so far, misbehaviour will still happen. It'll probably happen less, and be less prolonged and problematic, but it will still happen. This chapter, then, is what to do when it does – that is, how to intervene quickly, efficiently and effectively.

Note that while the interventions in this chapter are described individually, many will work in combination. Nor are you expected to use them all: just use one or two (or occasionally three) to nudge the student back on track. If the strategies don't work, then you either **Give a Warning** (Tip 77) or issue a sanction (Chapter 9).

Tip 59. QDL Corrections

QDL stands for 'quickly, discreetly and lightly', and by default that's how you want to correct student misbehaviour. It's an intervention approach that de-escalates situations, makes distractions less likely and doesn't limit your options should problems reoccur.

It also avoids an unwanted normalisation effect. When you keep on drawing attention to misbehaviour or allow it to draw attention to itself, you tell your students that misbehaviour is a common feature in your classroom. That's not a message you want to give because the more you give it, the more it becomes a reality.

Of course, there will be times when a correction needs to be towards the other end of the continuum (slow, obvious and strong), but even then you should still aim to keep it as quick, discreet and light as possible.

Tip 60. Pretend the Best

This is where you deal with the misbehaviour by pretending it's not misbehaviour:

- *Ahmed, you haven't started. Do you need my help?*
- *I can see you're struggling to find a book, Bethany. I'll look with you.*
- *Anissa, you seem lost in thought. Which question has caught your attention?*

An important caveat: pretend once, not twice. If the misbehaviour repeats, then you need to address it directly, such as using a **Discreet Direction** (Tip 71). If it repeats a third time, then you have a pattern and that needs a stronger response. Now it's either a warning (Tip 77) or a sanction (Chapter 9).

Tip 61. Ask a Casual Question

Ask the misbehaving student a (seemingly) casual question to refocus their attention:

- *How's the work going, Jamie?*
- *Carly, are you stuck?*
- *Selma, you seem confused. Everything okay?*

Strategic Corrections

The student will most likely say that everything is fine and will immediately get on with their work. Or they'll tell you they're stuck, which is also good because now you can give support and get them back on track.

Tip 62. Drop a Name

This is where you say ('drop') a student's name to show that you are aware of their current behaviour:

- *When we begin a sentence, we always use a capital letter – don't we Fran.*
- *When we go to the library, Anthony, we'll be walking in pairs and in silence.*
- *The questions I want you to do, George, are questions three to seven.*

Tip 63. Move Closer

Move closer to the student and stay there. This will almost certainly stop the misbehaviour straightaway and prevent it from reoccurring. You don't have to say anything, though you can if you want. The active element is proximity. When the work engages the student, then you can move away.

Do not let the brevity of this tip bely its power. It's simple, effective and confident.

Tip 64. Distract with an Activity

Distract the misbehaving student with a simple activity, such as tidying a pile of books or cleaning the whiteboard. This gives three wins. First, it acts as a misbehaviour circuit breaker. Second, it makes it easy to speak to the student discreetly. Third, it gives the other students the opportunity to refocus on their work, and therefore, they'll be less likely to act as an audience when the student sits back down. Any activity around a minute works well.

Tip 65. Use a Facial Expression

The three most useful facial expressions are quizzical, surprised and shocked. A Paddington Bear hard stare (an intense fixed frown) can also be useful if someone has forgotten their manners – thank you, Aunt Lucy. Whatever expression you use, the more exaggerated it is, the more likely it is to be noticed and understood.

Pulling a face often combines well with the next tip, **Give a Gesture**.

Tip 66. Give a Gesture

Common gestures include:

- Finger to lips to indicate silence.
- Rising upwards palm to indicate stand up.
- Raised and shown palm to indicate stop.
- Wagging finger to indicate no.
- Shaking of head to indicate no.

Teachers will also have gestures for 'open your book', 'start writing', 'close your book', 'look at me' and even 'put the chewing gum in the bin'.

Gestures are useful because they are non-distracting and, generally speaking, easy to understand. Their downside is that the student needs to be looking at you for them to work. If they're not, then either **Move Closer** (Tip 63) or stand in their line of sight. Alternatively, crisply say their name out loud and then give the correcting gesture.

Strategic Corrections

Tip 67. Bracket with Praise

This is where you praise nearby students for the behaviour you want to see. For example, if Petra hasn't started working yet, you can say something like this to the students sitting on either side of her:

Grace, great effort and focus. And you too, Victor. Your pen hasn't stopped writing!

Your praise may or may not be that important to Petra, but it becomes more important when students near to her are praised and she isn't. Hence, it prompts Petra to start working. When Petra has demonstrated appropriate behaviour, you can give her some praise, but don't give it too quickly. Remember, **Prised Praise Is Prized** (Tip 34).

Tip 68. Abrupt Stop

This is where you abruptly stop talking mid-sentence and wait for the misbehaviour to stop. It must be an abrupt stop, too, not one where you simply tail off. It's the abruptness together with the silence that follows that catches the attention of the misbehaving student.

You can increase the strength of an abrupt stop by adding a quizzical or shocked look (see **Pull a Face**, Tip 65). When you have compliance, hold the look for a beat and then crisply continue where you left off. Make sure your gaze settles on the student once or twice more so they know you haven't forgotten about them.

Tip 69. Public Anonymous

Here you identify the misbehaviour, but not who's misbehaving:

- *Year 12s, I can hear talking.*
- *Puffins, I need everyone looking my way.*
- *Books closed ... waiting for two ... waiting for one.*

Tip 70. Students in This Classroom

This is a variation of the previous tip. The difference is that you always begin with the phrase 'students in this classroom', and then you state rather than imply the correct behaviour:

- *Students in this classroom put up their hand and wait patiently to be chosen.*
- *Students in this classroom enter in silence and start working straightaway.*
- *Students in this classroom are silent when someone is reading out their work.*

By describing how students generally behave, you are leveraging a combination of social norms and social proof (see **Introduction: Conformity**).

Tip 71. Discreet Direction

This is where you move closer to the misbehaving student, lower your voice to something approaching a whisper and explicitly state the behaviour you want or don't want to see:

- *Paula, eyes on me when I'm talking.*
- *Darren, pen down. Thank you.*
- *Girls, no talking.*

If you want to say something lengthier, get the class occupied with work (e.g. a paired discussion for 30 seconds) and then speak to the misbehaving student:

> *Ilaria, when I was explaining to the class, you weren't looking at me. In fact, you were looking towards the back of the classroom.*

Strategic Corrections

Track me when I talk. It helps with listening and shows me you're paying attention. Thank you.

Do not stay around for a response. Simply state clearly what needs to happen and then walk away. Doing this assumes compliance.

Tip 72. Closed Choice

A Closed Choice is where one of the options is more favourable than the other:

- *Chloe, do you want to do the maths questions now or during break?*
- *Gabby, would you like to stand next to me and watch the game, or would you prefer to play kindly with Mimi?*
- *Faisal, would you like to help Simon tidy the work area now, or would you like to do it at the end of the lesson on your own?*

If Chloe, Gabby and Faisal make poor choices, then you must follow through with the less favourable option, even if it's less favourable to you (for instance, missing a bit of your break). Closed Choice only works if you mean it.

Tip 73. Name and Describe

This is where you name the student and describe the misbehaviour:

- *William, your book is open.*
- *Lucy, you are holding your pen.*
- *Annie, your bag is on your desk.*

Avoid adding other words like 'again' or 'always'. You are giving a neutral description of the student's behaviour and nothing more. Use a matter-of-fact tone.

Tip 74. Name and Instruct

This is where you name the student and give an instruction:

- *William, close your book.*
- *Lucy, put your pen down.*
- *Annie, put your bag on the floor.*

As with the previous tip, use a matter-of-fact tone.

Tip 75. Broken Record

This is where you deliver an instruction a maximum of three times. Aim for clarity, certainty and increasing pressure.

After the first instruction, give the student take-up time by busying yourself with something (e.g. handing out a resource, doing a default scan, helping a student, etc.). Most students will comply either right away or during the take-up time.

If the student doesn't comply, repeat the instruction but with more force. Have a little sharpness in your tone and add a quizzical or shocked look.

In the unlikely event that the student still doesn't comply, stand in front of the student, repeat the instruction and wait. Don't raise your voice or get drawn into a conversation. **Calm and Collected** (Tip 7) is the approach to take. If a student wants to discuss the instruction with you, tell them they can do so at the end of the lesson, but for now they must follow the instruction.

If the student doesn't comply, either **Give a Warning** (Tip 77) or issue a sanction (Chapter 9). And even if they do comply, make sure there's a **Follow-Up Conversation** (Chapter 10). This could range from a simple reminder of the expected behaviour or something more involved, depending on context.

Tip 76. Tactical Ignore

Let's say you're explaining an activity and a couple of students are quietly chatting. You could, of course, intervene right away. There is nothing wrong in doing that. But it might be better to get the class working and engaged, and then go and deal with the chatting students. By tactically ignoring the misbehaviour, you maintain the attention of the rest of the students, and you don't interrupt your explanation.

It can also be helpful to tactically ignore what's called 'secondary misbehaviour'. That's things like eye-rolling, huffing and puffing, smacking of lips and under-the-breath comments, including those under-the-breath comments that contain naughty words. Invariably, these behaviours are about saving face. Unfortunately, though, they're also the behaviours that can easily wind you up. Therefore, make sure you stay focused on the primary misbehaviour, which was the reason for the intervention in the first place, and then at a later point (e.g. the end of the lesson) follow up on the secondary misbehaviour. And makes sure you do, too: Tactical Ignore is only ever a temporary strategy.

A caveat: never ignore dangerous behaviour. That must be dealt with right away.

Tip 77. Give a Warning

If it's your choice to make (i.e. the behaviour policy leaves it to you to decide), limit yourself to one warning. Multiple warnings take away the certainty of the sanction and therefore reduce any **Deterrent Effect** (Chapter 13).

Nor should you feel obliged to give a warning. If it's the same misbehaviour from the same student every lesson, then a warning is not always necessary. In fact, it might even be counterproductive: the student clearly knows the misbehaviour is wrong so there's no reason why you can't go straight to the sanction. What you should do, though, is remind the student of the expected behaviour *before* the lesson begins (e.g. in the corridor). We look at how to do this in **Commitment Remind** (Tip 89).

Also, say the word 'warning' or use a clear synonym. Don't leave the student in any doubt that if the misbehaviour continues, a sanction will follow:

- *Glen, if you chat again, you will move seats. That's your warning.*
- *Nadia, if you fail to complete your homework again, it's an automatic detention. That's your warning.*
- *Steven, you are disrupting the learning of others. One more time and you'll be last to leave.*

Lastly, give the warning as unobtrusively as possible. A brief, quiet word is best. If you must deliver it publicly, do so quickly and crisply to reduce the time the spotlight is on the student. Also, use a matter-of-fact tone, the same tone you would use when telling someone that salad is good for them or that Paris is the capital of France. Don't stay around for a discussion either. Give it and move on. If the warning is not heeded, follow through with the sanction.

One Other Thing ...

If you use an intervention I haven't listed that works for you (i.e. it quickly gets the student back on track with minimal fuss), then carry on using it. If it works, it works. By the way, I'd love to hear about that strategy so please do send me an email and let me know about it. If I include it in a future edition of this book, I'll be sure to credit you.

9 Successful Sanctions

Prevention and intervention are not always enough. Sometimes the severity or repetition of the misbehaviour means that a line has been crossed and a sanction is needed. This chapter will not tell you where that line is or what the sanction should be – that's the job of the school behaviour policy – but it will give you four principles to make those sanctions more effective.

Tip 78. Certain Sanctions

Certain sanctions create a **Deterrent Effect** (Chapter 13). When a student is certain that misbehaviour will result in a sanction, the likelihood of misbehaviour reduces. But if they aren't certain, perhaps because the sanction is vague or inconsistently applied, then the deterrent effect is reduced and so the likelihood of misbehaviour increases.

Tip 79. Timely Sanctions

Timely sanctions have two benefits. First, they strengthen the psychological link between the misbehaviour and the consequence, that is, that the former caused the latter. The longer the delay, however, the weaker that link becomes. It follows, then, that getting a student to stay behind for two minutes at the end of the lesson will help to strengthen that link in a way that an hour's detention at the end of the week won't.

Second, timely sanctions leverage something called **Present Bias** (Chapter 13). We tend to put more value on what's just about to happen than what's going to happen in the future. The detention at the end of the week is more severe than the two minutes at the end of the lesson, but the former won't happen for a while so its influence is proportionately less. Conversely, the two minutes at the end of the lesson is not severe at all, but because it's just about to happen, its influence is proportionately greater.

To be clear: I am not against detentions. Detentions and all other commonly used sanctions (including internal exclusion, suspension and permanent exclusion) are a wholly legitimate response to misbehaviour. The issue is always context. Nevertheless, the principle of timeliness is a good one and should always be borne in mind.

Tip 80. Fair Sanctions

Sanctions should always be fair (i.e. proportionate, reasonable and consistent). Not only is this an ethical requirement, but it's also pragmatically useful. If a sanction is fair, then it's more likely to be accepted without argument. There might be some grumbling, but full-on arguing is rare. But if the sanction is harsh or unjust, then the student will likely (and rightly) feel aggrieved. At best, they'll put in less effort; at worst, they'll become disruptive.

The principle of fair sanctions links to the previous two tips. If a sanction is certain (Tip 78), then fair warning is built in – the student knows the sanction will happen because you've made that crystal clear. And if the sanction is timely (Tip 79), then it doesn't need to be severe because its strength comes from its speediness.

Tip 81. Dispassionate Sanctions

When you issue a sanction, take all emotions out of the delivery. Don't raise your voice, don't show irritation and don't say anything that you might later regret. Instead, use a calm and matter-of-fact approach.

Also, don't get involved in a discussion. If the student wants to discuss the sanction with you, tell them that they'll need to come back outside of lesson time. Lessons are for learning.

One Other Thing ...

Quick question: when was the last time you read the school behaviour policy? If it was more than three months ago, go and find it and read it again. Here's the thing, when you know the policy in detail, it makes it so much easier to issue sanctions that are certain, fair, timely and dispassionate – that is, sanctions that are more likely to get the student back on track and stop the misbehaviour reoccurring.

# 10 Follow-Up Conversation

A follow-up conversation is a one-to-one meeting with a student following a behaviour incident. This conversation must always take place if a sanction is given or if the misbehaviour has happened before. Its purpose is to stop the misbehaviour happening again, or at least to make it less likely. Usually, half a minute to a few minutes is enough.

Tip 82. Depersonalise the Misbehaviour

Make sure you take a depersonalised approach. The problem is the misbehaviour, not the student, so don't say things like this:

> *Jonny, you are so noisy, distracting everyone with your constant chatting.*

Instead, say something like this:

> *Jonny, chatting is distracting and gets in the way of learning. That's why it's against our classroom rules.*

If you take a depersonalised approach, the student will be more open to what you say. Also, you'll be less like to trigger a **Fight-or-Flight Response** (Chapter 13).

Follow-Up Conversation

Tip 83. Sidestep Defensiveness

While most students accept responsibility for their actions straight-away, some occasionally don't. For those who don't, avoid getting into a 'yes you did/no I didn't exchange', and instead use what they do accept and build from there.

Let's say that Jonny (from the previous tip) is adamant he wasn't chatting. He tells you that he knows it's wrong, but it simply wasn't him who was doing it [point of fact: it was]. You can sidestep his defensiveness by saying something like this:

> *It's good that you know that chatting is wrong. I agree with you, it is. Now give me a reason why it's wrong. What's the problem with it?*

Jonny might never admit his involvement, but it doesn't entirely matter. He's accepted that chatting is against the rules and you've prompted him to give you a reason why it's unacceptable, which he'll probably give. These are behaviour management wins. You've also leveraged the **Fear of Losing Face** (Chapter 13). It's embarrassing to say that something is wrong and then to be caught doing that very thing [obviously this doesn't apply to politicians].

Tip 84. Actively Listen

You don't have to agree, but you do have to listen to the student. First, it's respectful. Second, it might lead to some very important information. And third, to return the favour, it makes it much likely that the student will listen to you. Hence, they'll be more likely to be open to your behavioural expectations. For more on this, see the **Rule of Reciprocity** (Chapter 13).

Tip 85. Generate Buy-In

Generate buy-in from the student to change their behaviour. To do that, use one or more of the following appeals:

- Fair play.
- Duty.
- Self-interest.
- Concern for others.

Fair Play

Get the student to think about the purpose and helpfulness of rules (the analogy of a football game can work well here), and then get them to apply that thinking to classroom rules. What would it be like if every student behaved as they behaved? How much learning would happen? How easy would it be for students to focus on their work? How easy would it be for you to do your job and teach?

Duty

Get the student to think about their right to be respected and, from there, their duty to respect others. The golden rule is a helpful starting point: treat others the way you want to be treated. Ask them how respect and disrespect are shown in the classroom, and then get them to consider whether their behaviour was respectful or not.

Self-Interest

Get the student to think about how their misbehaviour affects them personally. What do they miss out on when they misbehave? What impact does it have on their learning? What are the immediate,

Follow-Up Conversation

medium and long-term losses? Pay particular attention to immediate losses because they carry more psychological weight (Chapter 13).

Concern for Others

Get the student to think about the impact of their behaviour on others. What do their peers think and feel when their learning is interrupted? What impact might their behaviour have on you, the teacher? What might the teaching assistant, form tutor, headteacher, etc. think and feel?

You can also get the student to think about the impact of their misbehaviour on loved ones. For instance, what would it be like for their mum (or dad, nan, uncle, carer, etc.) to receive a phone call from the school regarding their behaviour? What might that person think and feel? Why would they think and feel these things? What might they do or not do? This is a powerful approach which should not be used straightaway, but if the misbehaviour continues, then it's appropriate.

Tip 86. Prompt Commitment

Prompt a commitment from the student to change their behaviour. Ask a question like this:

> *So, given all that we've talked about, how will your behaviour be different in future lessons?*

Their answer might need some extra work (a bit of tweaking here and there), but essentially this is their commitment to change.

Tell them, too, that you are going to share their commitment with appropriate adults (i.e. their designated teaching assistant, head of year, form tutor, etc.). Explain that those adults can offer support and that by sharing their commitment it makes it more likely that they will stick to it (see Commitment Effect, Chapter 13).

Tip 87. Plan a Plan

This is an optional step. If it's the first time the student has misbehaved in this way, a simple commitment not to repeat the misbehaviour is probably enough. But if it has happened before or if was sufficiently problematic, then a plan is necessary.

The plan can take any form. If it's a single issue, then an **If-Then** (Tip 95) works well. Otherwise, use a series of clear and concrete steps or statements. For instance, let's say that a student is a bit excitable at the beginning of lessons, their plan might look like this:

- I am calm before I enter the classroom.
- I pick up my exercise book without talking to any other student.
- I start the Do Now activity straightaway.
- I don't make eye contact with any other student during the Do Now.

Limit the list to four behaviours to make the plan doable.

If things don't go according to plan, get the student to think about why it didn't and what needs to be different next time, then adapt the plan accordingly. Keep the sanction in place, however – sanctions work when they are certain, and commitments work when there are sanctions.

Tip 88. End on Good Terms

End the follow-up conversation on good terms to show that you don't hold a grudge and that your relationship with the student is still in good working order. If you can't end on good terms, don't

Follow-Up Conversation

end on bad terms. You must not give the student a justifiable reason to dislike you.

Tip 89. Commitment Remind

At the beginning of the next lesson, it is vital that you privately remind the student of their commitment to change. This is an example of **Just-in-Time Reminding** (Tip 22). It puts the commitment right at the front of the student's mind, reduces wriggle room and shows that you are a teacher who is on top of behaviour.

You can also flip this process and get the student to remind you:

> *Jonny, when I spoke to you yesterday, you told me that you were going to change your behaviour in my lessons. Remind me, what was your commitment? What exactly did you say?*

This gets Jonny to actively think about his commitment and what he must do to regulate his behaviour.

One Other Thing …

The follow-up conversation might trigger some feelings of guilt from the student. That's no bad thing. Guilt is an evolutionary setting that stops us behaving badly. Sure, there are unhelpful and unhealthy levels of guilt, but that's not what we are talking about here. We are talking about students recognising that they have behaved poorly and feeling the pang of regret for doing that. It's that emotional realisation that changes behaviour.

# 11 Managing the Challenging

Every class tends to have one or two (or more) students with challenging behaviour. This chapter is to help you manage those students. It needs to be stressed, though, that all the other tips in this book will also help. Simply put, they act together to raise the norm of acceptable classroom behaviour, and that new norm influences the behaviour of every single student, including the more challenging ones. To put it another way, a rising tide lifts all boats.

Tip 90. Do Something Nice

Do something nice for the student and chances are, due to a phenomenon known as the **Rule of Reciprocity** (Chapter 13), the student will want to do something nice in return. This is particularly the case when that nice thing is viewed as an act of kindness rather than duty, and it is specific to the student rather than a blanket nice thing for the whole class.

This nice thing doesn't have to be anything big. Taking an extra step to sort out a pastoral issue or just lending your pencil sharpener without being asked can be enough to trigger the effect. And once triggered, to return the favour, the student is more likely to work harder and behave better.

Three caveats: don't say you are doing the student a favour, don't expect anything back and don't be fawning. Do any of those things and the favour stops being a favour.

Tip 91. Get a Favour

To improve your relationship with a student, get that student to do you a favour. This paradoxical outcome is due to a phenomenon known as the **Ben Franklin Effect** (Chapter 13). Essentially, the effect creates cognitive dissonance, and that dissonance prompts the student to conclude that if they are doing you a favour, then they must like you. The favour can be anything from helping you carry some resources to solving an IT-related problem (even though you already know what to do!).

Tip 92. Find a Connection

It really doesn't matter what that connection is but find one. Perhaps you follow the same football team, play the same computer game, watch the same Netflix series, like the same author, listen to the same singer or find the same comedian funny. Maybe you were born in the same town, speak the same second language or play the same musical instrument. It might even be that you both keep goldfish, grow cacti or like Earl Grey tea. It doesn't really matter what the connection is, it just matters that you find one. And when you find it, keep on returning to it, because when you do that will improve your relationship with the student. Here's the thing: we tend to like people who are like us or like the things that we like, so leverage that hardwired setting and find that connection.

Tip 93. No, Because

When you say 'no' to the student, add the word 'because' and then give a reason that links to the student's best interest. For example:

- *No, because I want you to get more out of this lesson.*
- *No, because I believe you can do it.*
- *No, because I want you to develop this skill.*
- *No, because your progress is important to me.*
- *No, because I want the best for you.*

The 'no' is clear, definite and confident, while the explanation shows that you care about the student's best interests.

Tip 94. Find Out

Find out what approaches work and don't work with the student. Good sources of information are the previous teacher, the teaching assistant, the Special Educational Needs Coordinator, the form tutor and the head of year. Keep up to speed with SEND updates, too, if that applies.

You should also share any approach that works for you. Chances are, if it works for you, it will work for others too. It also allows for consistency across the staff group – remember, behaviour management is a team sport, and as such everyone needs to be pulling in the same direction.

Tip 95. If-Then

An If-Then is an individualised routine to help a specific student deal with a single problematic behaviour. It has the following underlying structure:

 If X happens, then do Y.

X is the problem and Y is the solution.

Managing the Challenging

To be effective, as with all routines, the If-Then needs to be a habitual response. In other words, it needs to be neurologically encoded to the point that when X happens, the student automatically thinks and follows through with the Y.

It's not possible to have an exhaustive list of If-Thens (it depends on the individual student), but here are some examples to show how it works:

- If I want to chat to Tommy, then I'll tell myself 'STOP!'
- If Tommy starts chatting to me, then I'll tell him not to and I'll get on with the work.
- If I want to call out, then I'll put up my hand and wait patiently in silence.
- If I want to pick up another student's belongings, then I'll pick up my pen instead.
- If I want to make an unkind comment, then I'll tell myself to be nice.
- If I want to walk out of the classroom, then I'll count backwards from a 100 in sevens to calm myself down. If I still want to walk out, then I will put up my hand and speak to the teacher or teaching assistant.
- If I want to ask a question and I've already asked three, then I will wait to the end of the lesson and ask the teacher one-to-one.
- If I want to give up, then I will try three more times. If I've tried three more times, then I will raise my hand and wait for the teacher to help me.

To help the encoding process, at the start of every lesson, remind the student of their If-Then strategy – or, better still, get the student to remind you. Be discreet and encouraging, and don't stop until the problem behaviour has itself consistently stopped.

Also, make sure you view any setback not as a failure but as a stage in the learning process. Replacing one habit with another takes time.

Tip 96. Define and Grade

This is a game-like activity that also gets the student to think deeply about their behaviour. There are two parts to it:

- Define success.
- Grade success.

Define Success

Explain in detail what the student needs to do to have a successful lesson. This is their success criteria. Aim for a maximum of four items to make it a manageable target. For example:

- You write down the date and title straightaway.
- You put up your hand and wait patiently to be chosen.
- You don't talk to Charlie for the entire lesson.
- You always look forward.

Grade Success

At the end of the lesson, grade the student on how well they did in meeting the success criteria. Give a whole number out of ten (ten equals perfection), write it on a bit of paper and then turn that paper over so it's face down. Then get the student to guess the number you wrote, but they only get one attempt. Keep this process going every lesson until the student can guess the number correctly three times in a row.

The student's first guess is likely to be unrealistically positive. You might have graded them as, say, a three and yet they grade themselves as a nine. Therefore, you need to explain in detail why you

Managing the Challenging

graded them as you did, making sure you link your observations to the success criteria. For example:

You were slow to write down the date and title. You were slow because you talked to Charlie. You looked back at least four times. And when you put your hand up to answer a question, while it was good that you were silent, you weren't patient. You were putting your hand up as high as possible, even raising up from your chair a little. You also spoke to Charlie on one other occasion.

Over time the student will get better at guessing correctly – which means, in effect, they get better at seeing their behaviour through your eyes. But you must make sure you always give the grade you truly believe and always detail the behaviour you saw, linking it explicitly to the success criteria.

One Other Thing …

There can be a temptation to lower your expectations for challenging students. Don't do it. Sure, be encouraging, be supportive and provide self-management strategies, but don't lower your expectations. If you do, you'll make it harder for the student to behave appropriately, not easier. At the same time, your job will become much more difficult. Remember, behaviour moves in the direction of the expectation, so keep those expectations consistently high. All students need you to do this, but challenging students need you to do it even more.

12 Never-Evers

Effective behaviour management isn't just about doing the right things but also about not doing the wrong things. Doing the wrong things can cause misbehaviour to spiral out of control, relationships to be trashed and patterns of problematic behaviour to become the norm – hence, the importance of this chapter and its various never-evers.

Tip 97. Never Shout

Shouting at students is entirely unethical and that's reason enough never to do it. It's also counterproductive. First, the students might shout back. That's particularly true if the students come from environments where shouting is the norm. Second, it makes you an unlikeable person. Consequently, the students will be less likely to work for you and follow your instructions. Third, it can cause some students to become nervous or anxious, which can impact learning and mental health. Hence, don't do it.

In the very short term, shouting can rapidly stop misbehaviour. That, of course, is its appeal. But due to the law of diminishing returns, it quickly loses its impact. In fact, over time, shouting ends up as little more than white noise. It blurs into the background, and along with it so does the teacher's standing and authority.

Raising your voice to get student attention is different from shouting, so it's fine. Just make sure there's no anger or other negative emotion involved, and your volume comes down straightaway.

In the same vein, don't humiliate, be sarcastic or make a joke at a student's expense. In short, be pleasant and polite – which is one-half of being a **Nice Boss** (Tip 6).

Tip 98. Never Argue

Arguing doesn't resolve situations. It either entrenches positions or, worse, causes behaviour to spiral out of control. Also, if you're arguing, then you are not **Calm and Collected** (Tip 7), which is the opposite of what you always want to be.

If a student wants to argue with you, say that you are happy to discuss the matter at break but not during the lesson. Chances are, they won't turn up, but even if they do, they'll be calmer. If the student arrives with friends, send the friends away and speak to the student one-to-one.

Tip 99. Never Say Please

Well, you can if you want, but it's more effective to say 'thank you'. Both 'please' and 'thank you' are equally polite, but the former has a begging quality, whereas the latter assumes and therefore prompts compliance. You can see the relative strength of each when you put them side by side:

- *Eyes on me, please/Eyes on me, thank you.*
- *Pens down, please/Pens down, thank you.*
- *Please queue in a straight line/Queue in a straight line, thank you.*

If you hear yourself saying 'please', train yourself to say 'thank you'.

Tip 100. Never Turn a Blind Eye

It doesn't matter what it is or where it happens – classroom, corridor, school hall, playground, school gates, etc. – you must always respond to misbehaviour. If you don't, if you turn a blind eye, your students will conclude that you are either scared of them or a bit inept. Neither is a helpful conclusion.

Tip 101. Never Break Your Word

If you say you're going to speak to a student at break, be in your classroom waiting. If you say you're going to issue a sanction, issue it. If you say you're going to the school play on Thursday night, be there. If, for some genuine and unforeseen reason, you can't do what you've said you're going to do, address it at the next opportunity and be doubly sure that you don't break your word again with that student.

Tip 102. Never Have Favourites

Students must not think that you value one of their peers more than you value them. The unfairness of that hurts and invariably will damage the teacher-student relationship. So don't have any favourites – or, if you do, don't show that you do. This might require some acting by you, but it is a part worth playing.

Tip 103. Never Take It Personally

The student is a child. Maybe a very young child, maybe an older child, but either way a child. They are still under development, still a work in progress, still growing up. So don't take their misbehaviour personally – especially if it was meant personally, which sometimes it is. All it reflects is their level of maturity.

Tip 104. Never Issue a Warning Like a Threat

Do so and you are likely to trigger a **Fight-or-Flight Response** (Chapter 13). Some students will go into fight mode, and as such be more likely to shout, swear and get angry, whereas others will go into flight mode, with panic and anxiety taking over.

Tip 105. Never Be Friends with Students

You are the students' teacher. When you become anything other than their teacher, you blur the edges of that role and confuse your students. The teacher-student relationship becomes a mess because, in effect, it stops being a teacher-student relationship. You lose authority. You lose respect. You lose effectiveness. Sure, be friendly, but never be a friend. It's inappropriate, unprofessional and counterproductive.

Tip 106. Never Let Students Work Off Sanctions

A student is misbehaving in your lesson. The sanction, which you've stated clearly, is that they spend five minutes of their breaktime with you. However, ten minutes before the lesson bell, you tell the student that if they're well behaved for the rest of the lesson, then some or all of that time can be worked off.

This approach seems like a win-win. You get a better-behaved student and you don't lose any of your breaktime. What's not to like?

Unfortunately, it's a lose-lose. The problem is you've undermined the effectiveness of the sanction by taking away its certainty and thus made it more likely that the student will misbehave next lesson. You've also shown the student and the class that you are not a person of your word. For sanctions to be effective, they must be certain (see **Certain Sanctions**, Tip 78).

Tip 107. Never Accept Answers Shouted Out

If you do, you'll train your students to answer in that way. In fact, don't even acknowledge the student. Instead, keep on repeating the question until a student answers in the correct way, and then praise the student for how they answered. It doesn't even have to be the correct answer.

If shouting out continues, then increase the strength of the correction by using strategies such as **Public Anonymous** (Tip 69) or **Discreet Direction** (Tip 71). If it happens a further time, **Give a Warning** (Tip 77) or issue a sanction (Chapter 9). At the start of the next lesson, remind all students of the correct routine.

Tip 108. Never Take Questions Mid-Message

You are giving an instruction or an explanation and halfway through a student puts up their hand to ask a question. By default, don't take that question. The problem is that one question can become two, and two can become three, and in no time you lose the attention of the entire class. Worse, chatting fills the void that the exchange creates. Also, chances are, the next thing you were going to say would've answered the question anyway.

Instead, place the questioner on hold and continue speaking. Use a simple gesture such as a raised palm so you don't disturb your flow. When you've finished speaking, that's when you can (quickly) deal with questions, but even then it's often best to get the rest of the class working first.

Tip 109. Never Lend a Pen

Every time you do, you lower your expectations and thus make it more likely that the student won't have a pen next time.

What you can do, though, is help the student come up with a plan to make sure the pen problem doesn't reoccur. In other words, don't lend a pen, but lend a hand.

A caveat: you must always make reasonable adjustments so that all students can access learning. For some students, this may also include the provision of a pen. That said, for the vast majority of students, the tip holds true. Lend a hand, not a pen.

Tip 110. Never Allow Chatting

Chatting is counterproductive to learning and only ever leads to more chatting and other off-task behaviours. Work-related talking is another matter, of course, and if it's been authorised by you and it aids the learning process, then it's fine. But when it comes to chatting, don't allow it.

Tip 111. Never Distract

Never distract students when they are working. If you must do something potentially distracting (e.g. talk to a student, walk around the classroom or hand out resources), do so as unobtrusively as possible. Don't break the under-the-spell state of a focused class.

Tip 112. Never Give a Whole-Class Sanction

A whole-class sanction is as unethical as it is counterproductive. It will unite those who weren't misbehaving with those who were, and so has the potential to turn the classroom into a 'you versus them' battlefield.

Tip 113. Never Use External Rewards

On the face of it, external rewards such as well-done badges, gold stars or postcards home seem like a good idea, not least because they can give a quick boost to student motivation. Unfortunately, though, they can also quickly become problematic.

First, the reward can act as a distraction. Instead of focusing on the task, the students focus on the reward and that gets in the way of

Brilliant Behaviour in 60 Seconds or Less

learning. Second, it sends an unhelpful message. It tells the students that the work lacks sufficient intrinsic value. Third, it can leverage something called the **Overjustification Effect** (Chapter 13). When you reward students for things they already like doing, their intrinsic motivation tends to reduce. Worse, when you remove the reward, which at some point you'll have to do, that intrinsic motivation can be slow to return to previous levels, if it returns at all.

If you do intend to use rewards, go for frugal and fast – in other words, don't use rewards often and don't use them for long. Alternatively, don't use them at all.

Tip 114. Never Let Life Interfere

You know that tricky stuff that's happening in your life? You know those worries you have about money or relationships or work or … well, whatever they are, none of that stuff has any right to be in your classroom, to influence your behaviour or unsettle your consistency. What's outside the classroom must stay outside the classroom. That's your professional duty.

Tip 115. Never Criticise the School

You are, of course, entitled to an opinion, but you are not allowed to share that opinion with students or parents if it's negative about the school. So, to be specific: never criticise the school culture, ethos or traditions; never criticise the school rules, routines or expectations; and never criticise any policy the school is putting into place. You must be a loyal promoter of the school.

If you find something wrong or intolerable, take it through the correct channels. In fact, you are morally obliged to do exactly that. But sharing your opinion with students or parents is not one of those channels.

One Other Thing …

Never ever read this book only once. What you take away from it today will not be what you'll take away from it in six weeks' time or six months' time – or, indeed, six years' time. Instead, dip in and out. You'll find different things when you do, and some of those things will be exactly what you need at the point when you need them.

13 Unconscious Processes

We like to see ourselves as rational and logical beings, capable of clear, reasoned decision-making and bestowed with freedom of choice. And, indeed, that represents some of what we are and what we have. Yet, for evolutionary reasons, not least the need to save time and energy and to get on with others, much of our behaviour is determined not by conscious thought but by unconscious processes.

This chapter will consider several of these processes and then map them onto various tips within this book. Doing this will help to explain why those tips are effective and, through that knowledge, allow you to be more effective in their use. When we understand how something works, we tend to have greater control over that thing – in this instance, a greater control over the context in which students make decisions.

Familiarity Heuristic/Status Quo Bias

These are two different yet overlapping effects. The Familiarity Heuristic is the tendency to do what we always do when we find ourselves in familiar situations, while Status Quo Bias is a preference for maintaining the current state of affairs. Both processes are underpinned by habit and inertia – that is, the more a behaviour is encoded into our neural networks, the more it becomes our default way of acting, to the point that to do anything different requires extra effort, so most of the time we don't bother.

These two effects link to any routine-based tip – so that's **Key Routines** (Chapter 6), **Attention Grabbers** (Chapter 7) and **If-Then** (Tip 95). Routines make specific responses so familiar that they become the default behaviour. In effect, appropriate behaviour becomes the easier option, and misbehaviour, the option that requires effort. And that, of course, is always the way you want it to be.

Confidence Heuristic

The more confident someone is, the more persuasive we find them. We use their confidence as a shortcut to assess whether they're right or not. Politicians know this, particularly those on the demagogue end of the spectrum, and teachers need to know it too for non-demagogue reasons. When you come across as confident, your students are more likely to believe in you, trust your judgements and follow your instructions. That in turn makes the classroom an easier place to manage.

The Confidence Heuristic informs every chapter in this book. That said, it is particularly important in **Clarity and Presence** (Chapter 3), **Attention Grabbers** (Chapter 7) and **Strategic Corrections** (Chapter 8).

Present Bias

Present Bias (also known as the time inconsistency problem) is the tendency to place more value on the present than on the future. It explains a great deal of human behaviour, including why eating doughnuts is more appealing than a slimmed-down body, why spending money on nights out is more appealing than saving for a rainy day and why scrolling through social media is more appealing than a tidy pile of completed marking. Now beats later.

This bias also helps to explain a great deal of student misbehaviour. For instance, the excitement of playing the class clown now beats the boredom of an after-school detention; the fun of chatting to your mate now beats the seriousness of a talk with the teacher at the end of the lesson; and the relief of not working hard now beats the disappointment of a poor final grade. The consequences are all negative, unpleasant and unwanted, but they will happen in the future, while the appealing behaviour is happening now.

Present Bias links to **QDL Corrections** (Tip 59) and **Timely Sanctions** (Tip 79). These two tips bring forward in time the consequences of the misbehaviour (i.e. the corrections and sanctions), and so their impact is more keenly felt or anticipated. It also links to **Start Line** (Tip 32) and **Deadline** (Tip 33) because both emphasise the importance of working in the now.

Fight-or-Flight Response

The Fight-or-Flight Response is our inbuilt survival mechanism. It is our evolved and automatic response to potentially injurious or life-threatening situations. It screams with certainty and demands that we act without hesitation to ensure our safety. It also has a hairline trigger and errs towards false positives, seeing dangers where they don't exist, or if they do exist, then exaggerating those dangers because being safe is better than being sorry.

Our Fight-or-Flight Response has served our species well – indeed, without it, extinction would have been a certainty. And it continues to be needed by those who live in more dangerous areas or experience dangerous events. But for teachers in the classroom, when left unchecked, this hardwired survival response tends to lead to disastrous outcomes and a great deal of professional regret. In fight mode, teachers are more likely to shout or say something unkind, and in flight mode, they are more likely to ignore misbehaviour, or at best intervene with insufficient confidence and timeliness. Either way, misbehaviour worsens and relationships become strained, perhaps even trashed.

It's not possible to turn the Fight-or-Flight Response off – it's always there, monitoring your senses, ready to act – but you can get better at regaining self-control, and you do that by using the strategies described in **Calm and Collected** (Tip 7). Also, the better you get at using those strategies, the less likely you are to lose self-control in the first place. In effect, the strategies become your hardwired response to misbehaviour.

The Deterrent Effect

The Deterrent Effect comes into play when two conditions are met. First, the student thinks their misbehaviour will be noticed, and second, they think a negative outcome will result (e.g. a follow-up conversation, a phone call home, a sanction, etc.). If either condition is missing, then the effect doesn't happen.

The Deterrent Effect has little to do with the severity of a sanction. If a student doesn't think they're going to get caught or that anything will happen even if they are, then severity is irrelevant. Conversely, if they think those two outcomes are certain, then severity isn't needed.

The Deterrent Effect links to **Withitness** (Tip 4) and **Certain Sanctions** (Tip 78) – the former because the withit teacher knows what's going on in their classroom and demonstrates that to the students, and the latter because, of course, the sanction is certain. In other words, the two tips satisfy the effect's two conditions.

The Overjustification Effect

Rewarding students for things they already like doing tends to undermine their intrinsic motivation. A possible explanation for this is that the student sees their enjoyment and satisfaction coming from the reward rather than the task itself; hence, intrinsic motivation drops. Further, when you remove the reward, which at some point you have to do, that intrinsic motivation can be slow to return to previous levels, assuming it ever does. This is the Overjustification Effect.

The effect links to **Never Use External Rewards** (Tip 113) and **Prised Praise Is Prized** (Tip 34), the latter because praise is a type of external reward. The general principle is that if you don't need to use rewards, then don't use them, and if you do use them, then use them sparingly.

The Pygmalion and Golem Effects

The Pygmalion and Golem Effects are different sides of the same self-fulfilling prophesy. The Pygmalion Effect is where a high expectation tends to lead to an increase in a person's performance, while the Golem Effect is the opposite, a low expectation leading to low performance.

The two effects work in the same circular way: your beliefs about a person influence how you act towards them, those actions influence how they see themselves, that self-view impacts their performance, that performance confirms your beliefs, those beliefs influence how you act towards them and so on in a self-reinforcing feedback loop.

Clearly, teachers need to leverage the Pygmalion and avoid the Golem. There are two ways to do that. First, you believe – fully, totally and utterly believe – that all of your students are capable of brilliant behaviour (which they are), and then you communicate that belief through your **Consistently High Expectations** (Tip 2). Second, if you don't believe it, then you must nevertheless *act* as though you

Unconscious Processes

do. In other words, you pretend and you stick with those same high expectations. The second method isn't as good as the first because it runs the risk of unconscious slippage (i.e. unintentionally communicating what you truly believe), but it's better than not acting it, so make sure you put in an Oscar-winning performance.

The Curse of Knowledge

The Curse of Knowledge (also known as the Curse of Expertise) is the assumption that other people will have the same background knowledge and level of understanding as you. In short, you think that what's clear to you will be clear to others. For teachers, this translates as a tendency to overestimate what the students already know and underestimate how long it will take them to learn something new, hence the epithet 'curse'.

The Curse of Knowledge links to **Just-in-Time Reminding** (Tip 22), **Check for Understanding** (Tip 24), **Narrate Compliance** (Tip 25), **Teach Your Routines** (Tip 37) and **Remind and Revisit** (Tip 40). In effect, you are countering an unhelpful assumption with a helpful one, namely that the students won't automatically know what to do and therefore will need to be taught multiple times.

Inattentional Blindness

Inattentional Blindness is failing to notice something in plain sight because your attention is elsewhere. Though normally a bad thing in a classroom, it can be our ally in one regard: when students are focused on their work, they tend not to notice behaviour that would otherwise be distracting, including misbehaviour from their peers. And if they don't notice those things, they don't engage with them.

Inattentional Blindness links to **The 100% Rule** (Tip 3) and **Clarity and Presence** (Chapter 3) because in both instances attention is directed to where it needs to be – towards the work or to the teacher.

The Scarcity Heuristic

The Scarcity Heuristic is where you perceive something as having more value because of its scarcity. Hence, you either want more of it or don't want to waste what you have.

This effect links to **Deadline** (Tip 33) and **Prised Praise Is Prized** (Tip 34). The former creates the scarcity of time, or at least the perception of scarcity, whereas the latter creates the scarcity of praise, or at least a reduction in its availability. Either way, the students work harder.

The Commitment Effect/Fear of Losing Face

The Commitment Effect and the Fear of Losing Face are closely connected. The former is the tendency to follow through with a commitment once it's been told to others, and the latter is the main driver of that tendency. Simply put, we don't want people to have a poor opinion of us, to think that we are not dependable, so we tend do what we said we were going to do. Both effects link to **Prompt Commitment** (Tip 86) particularly when there is a public element to that commitment.

Social Loafing

Social Loafing is the tendency to put in less effort when working as part of a group. It happens for several reasons including laziness, distraction and thinking your contribution isn't significant. Group behaviour can also be a factor. For instance, if others aren't working hard, the tendency is to sink to that level and join them. Conversely, if the group is very engaged, it's harder to find the space to contribute and so you give up trying.

As a rule of thumb, the larger the group, the greater the likelihood of this effect. Therefore, if you're going to put students into large groups, you need a good reason why and a clear plan to counter the inherent problems. If you don't have those two things, then don't do it.

Social Loafing works against the **The 100% Rule** (Tip 3) and **Peak Participation** (Tip 30). It's also the reason why 'rows and columns' is the most effective **Classroom Layout** (Tip 26). Not only does it favour individual and paired working, but it also reduces the likelihood of social interactions (aka social distractions).

The Rule of Reciprocity

When someone does something nice for us, we tend to want to do something nice in return. That's the Rule of Reciprocity. The rule has an obvious evolutionary benefit: if we all return favours, then everyone wins. This reciprocity idea has even entered our language in phrases such as 'give and take', 'one good turn deserves another' and 'you scratch my back, I'll scratch yours' – and woe betide us if we don't return the favour because 'what goes around comes around'.

The Rule of Reciprocity links most obviously to **Do Something Nice** (Tip 90). When you do a favour for a student, the student feels obliged to repay that nice thing, which normally means they work harder and behave better. Likewise when you **Actively Listen** (Tip 84) to the student, it makes it more likely that they will listen to you in return. It might also be a factor in **Nice Boss** (Tip 6) in that nice teachers are more likely to get nice students, as long as they are also the boss in the classroom.

The Ben Franklin Effect

Get someone to do you a favour, and there's a good chance they'll be more positive towards you, particularly if they didn't like you much to begin with. This paradoxical outcome is the Ben Franklin Effect. The most accepted explanation for this effect centres around cognitive dissonance. In other words, there is a tension between the behaviour (doing a favour) and the belief (I don't like that person), so to resolve that tension, the belief is changed. Hence, the receiver of the gift is liked.

The effect links most obviously to **Get a Favour** (Tip 91), but it also links to **Distract with an Activity** (Tip 64) because that activity is normally a 'favour' of some sort.

The Ovsiankina Effect

The Ovsiankina Effect refers to a motivational tendency to restart and complete interrupted tasks. The interruption creates psychological discomfort that can only be resolved by finishing what's been started. In a sense, the unfinished task is like an itch, and the completion of the task, a satisfying scratch.

An example of this effect was used in **Setting Homework** (Tip 48). Specifically, to increase homework completion rates, it can be useful to get students to start homework in class so they are more motivated to finish it at home. One or two minutes is enough to leverage the effect.

One Other Thing …

If you want to share these unconscious processes with your students, go ahead. It won't diminish their influence (such is their innate and hardwired nature), and, almost certainly, your students will find the material fascinating. Who knows – they might even develop a newfound respect for your behaviour management skills given the theory that underpins those skills.

14 Turn the Class Around

Our job as behaviour management practitioners is to normalise pro-social and pro-learning behaviours so that all students can flourish. That's what this book is all about. Sometimes, though, classroom culture shifts in the wrong direction and misbehaviour becomes the daily default. If that ever happens to you, the following six steps are a way to turn the class around and get your students back on track. It will require grit, determination and (maybe) a bit of bravery, but if you follow these steps, you can do it.

Step One – Admit and Commit

Admit that change needs to happen and then commit to making that change. As extra self-leverage, tell a colleague/friend/spouse/relative of your commitment. When we tell others that we are going to do something, we're more likely to do that thing.

Don't play the blame game, either. So don't blame the students, the students' parents, the school, the neighbourhood or the previous teacher. None of that is helpful. Instead, focus solely on what needs to be done.

Step Two – Tell It and Own It

Say something like this to the students (modify it to fit your context):

> *Behaviour is not as good as it needs to be in this class. The boundaries and conditions for learning are not in place and it is my responsibility to make sure they are. I don't think you are enjoying my lessons as much as you should either, which makes sense because learning and enjoyment go together.*

You won't be telling the students anything they don't know, but your directness and honesty will definitely get their attention. Add a pause for dramatic effect, and then say something like this:

> *But I'm going to put us back on track. I'm going to put those boundaries and conditions in place so I can teach and you can learn. Because that's my job. My job is to prioritise your learning.*

That last sentence is key. It's your mandate to teach, to take responsibility for student behaviour and to turn things around. You know it's true and just as importantly so do your students.

Step Three – Explain It

Choose three routines or expectations (the ones that are causing the most problems) and go through them *in detail*. They'll probably be no different from the routines and expectations that you started the year with, but do it anyway.

What does 'in detail' mean? It means back to front, inside out, upside down and from all angles. It means breaking down your expectations to their smallest instructional component.

Also, tell your students that you are going to follow the school behaviour policy to the letter. If a warning or sanction is required, you will give it calmly, respectfully and unfailingly.

Turn the Class Around

Make the point (and keep making the point) that your expectations set up the conditions for learning. Learning is their right to expect and your responsibility to ensure – there's your mandate again.

Step Four – Do It

Do what the behaviour policy says you should do when misbehaviour happens – because it will happen.

Let's say you've just finished going through your expectations in detail (Step Three), and almost immediately there's misbehaviour. What do you do? You do two things. First, you congratulate yourself on your good fortune. You've just been given an opportunity to show your students that you are a person of your word and you've not had to wait ages for it. Second, you do whatever the behaviour policy says you should do. If it's a warning, you give the warning; if it's a sanction, you give the sanction. What you mustn't do is turn a blind eye or give a second chance.

Step Five – Keep Doing It

Keep repeating Step Four. Consistency is the key. Use your **Nice Boss** (Tip 6) qualities of pleasant and polite and confident and assertive. Stay **Calm and Collected** (Tip 7) at all times.

Step Six – Believe It

You have to believe – truly believe! – that your students are capable of excellent behaviour. That's every single one of them. Because, you see, they are – completely, absolutely, fully, entirely and without any shadow of a doubt.

But perhaps your classroom culture has needed fixing for a while. Maybe, say, mucking around, rudeness and shoddy work have become the exhausting norm, and hence, you are certain that your class are a lost cause. Your cynicism, given your experience, is understandable. But it's also wrong and problematic. Here's the thing: if you don't believe your students can change, that they are capable of excellent behaviour, then your expectations will align accordingly, and the misbehaviour will stay fixed in place. So believe it.

If, however, you can't believe it, then you have one further option. It's the next step.

Step Seven – Act Like You Believe It

Act like you believe your students are capable of excellent behaviour. It's not as good as Step Six, because your true feelings might slip through, but it's the next best thing. It will need some forced make-believe on your part, but nevertheless do it. It's true anyway, so it won't do any harm. And if you can act convincingly, it could do a great deal of good.

One Other Thing …

Your students want you to turn the class around. Really, they do. Sure, some might've enjoyed the misbehaviour initially, and a few might put up a bit of resistance now that you're putting an end to it, but the majority will want you to turn the class around and get them back on track. In fact, they are desperate for that to happen for (at least) four reasons. First, misbehaviour is boring. Second, learning is fun. Third, they know they are wasting their time. Fourth, they want to be in a class where it is safe to learn. So turn that class around – it's what the students want you to do anyway.

Further Support

If you want more behaviour-related input from me, there are three options available to you: my online courses, in-person CPD, and conference keynotes and breakouts.

Online Courses

I have created three online courses:

- Better Behaviour – an in-depth five-week behaviour management course for teachers.
- Behaviour Boost – a one-week behaviour management course for teachers.
- Supporting Progress – a one-week course for academic and pastoral support staff.

Individuals can enrol through my website. Use these codes to get 10% off the price: **Better10**, **Boost10** and **Progress10**.

If you want to make a bulk booking for your school or cohort of schools, email me and I'll send through an invoice with the 10% reduction included.

Further Support

In-Person CPD

You can find details about my in-person CPD on my website.

Website: behaviourbuddy.co.uk

Conferences

I can deliver keynotes and breakout sessions. Email me for details.

Email: robin@behaviourbuddy.co.uk

For Product Safety Concerns and Information please contact our EU representative GPSR@taylorandfrancis.com
Taylor & Francis Verlag GmbH, Kaufingerstraße 24, 80331 München, Germany

www.ingramcontent.com/pod-product-compliance
Lightning Source LLC
Chambersburg PA
CBHW071743150426
43191CB00010B/1673